MANUFACTURING CONTROLS

How the Manufacturing Manager Can Improve Profitability

MANUFACTURING CONTROLS

CONTROLS

How the Manufacturing Manager Can Improve Profitability

MARTIN R. SMITH

VNR **VAN NOSTRAND REINHOLD COMPANY**
NEW YORK   CINCINNATI   ATLANTA   DALLAS   SAN FRANCISCO
LONDON   TORONTO   MELBOURNE

Van Nostrand Reinhold Company Regional Offices:
New York   Cincinnati   Atlanta   Dallas   San Francisco

Van Nostrand Reinhold Company International Offices:
London   Toronto   Melbourne

Library of Congress Catalog Card Number: 81-807
ISBN: 0-442-21942-3

Manufactured in the United States of America

Published by Van Nostrand Reinhold Company
135 West 50th Street, New York, N.Y. 10020

Published simultaneously in Canada by Van Nostrand Reinhold Ltd.

15 14 13 12 11 10 9 8 7 6 5 4 3 2 1

Library of Congress Cataloging in Publication Data

Smith, Martin R., 1934–
    Manufacturing controls.

    Includes index.
    1. Production control.   I. Title.
TS157.S62   658.5   81-807
ISBN 0-442-21942-3   AACR2

Introduction

"CONGRATULATIONS! YOU'RE NOW MANUFACTURING MANAGER FOR PMD"

You've just been appointed manufacturing manager for the Parts Manufacturing Division (PMD) of International Machinery Incorporated, and you are naturally quite elated. You want to get off to a fast start and go on to further successes with your new company. You are very enthusiastic about your new position but clear-headed enough to realize the extent of the challenge facing you.

You know that one of the first tasks you must perform is to seize control over operations so you are aware of how things are going at any moment in time, and how operations are progressing to the division's profit plan. You also understand that without the proper controls, danger spots such as high costs, poor productivity or overbudget expenses could quickly result in divisional losses for the quarter (enough to lose your job).

You have been around long enough to recognize the dangers of running a manufacturing operation without benefit of timely and effective controls over such important variables as headcount, inventory, overtime, and purchasing. Many are the times you have seen or heard of manufacturing managers who have bit the dust because of their inability to detect critical trends before it was too late.

You have vowed that would *never* happen to you! You are determined to establish and maintain those controls you know are necessary to ensure early detection of problems, so fast and potent corrective action can be applied.

This book will help you succeed. It focuses attention on those controls needed for every critical function of the manufacturing enterprise. Control techniques for materials, labor, equipment, and costs are described in detail. These techniques can be applied to almost any industry, if you, as manufacturing manager, will tailor them to your specific company. In many instances, the controls can be used as described exactly in this book. Use your judgment to make those decisions.

Whether you are a vice president of manufacturing, plant manager, foreman, or support supervisor (materials, quality, engineering, etc.) this book will help you understand the different functions of manufacturing, and it will allow you to see how they mesh to achieve profitable operations. Anybody working now in manufacturing or considering the possibility will learn a great deal from this book.

THE COMPANY YOU ARE WORKING FOR

The balance of this book will focus on a specific company to describe all of the techniques it uses to control manufacturing operations. The use of one company as the example for application of manufacturing controls will provide a source of continuity, and will make it easier to visualize all of the inter-relationships within manufacturing, as opposed to use of many different companies to make the same points.

The company you have just been hired by is International Machinery Incorporated,* and you are manufacturing manager for its Parts Manufacturing Division, consisting of three plants—all under your supervision.

International Machinery is a diversified company (some still call them conglomerates) whose divisions produce plastics machinery, oil field supplies, construction equipment, disposable medical supplies, and fabricated metal products.

Parts Manufacturing Division (PMD) manufactures oil field couplings and fittings, spare parts for use in plastics machinery, and stainless steel valves for petrochemical plants.

PMD's machine shop operations consist of automatic screw machines, centerless grinders, automatic chuckers, NC machining centers, threading and tapping machines, milling machines, drill presses,

*Fictitious, of course, although based on a composite of real companies.

and vertical boring mills. Its finishing operations specialize in heat treating, plating, painting, and embossing.

The assembly operations consist of assembly of stainless steel valves for sale to petrochemical plants and contractors as well as minor sub-assembly of spare parts for sale to International Machinery's plastics machinery division.

PMD manufactures to stock rather than to specific job orders. Couplings, fittings, and stainless steel valves are stocked in a variety of sizes and shapes while spare parts (a relatively small part of the business) are also manufactured to stock based on the forecasted needs of International Machinery's plastics machine division.

Total divisional sales is $45 million annually. PMD's headquarters and largest plant is located in Houston, Texas, with two smaller plants in Pittsburgh, Pennsylvania and Los Angeles, California.

Now that you're acquainted with PMD, let's move on to learn to use those controls which have made PMD successful.

and exhibit B will argue, fulfilling requirements specified in both teaching, learning and practice.
the benefits of ... transition of ... the ... physical ... and data sample to rationalize of things and ... regulate, as well as maintaining example, if possible, and factor role to future, and if finances, plates improvement through

Moreover, what appears, with ... that to exhibit's ... pains, through and stories that also are included in a study of how and ... help which provide a database around part of the business ... maintained to ... stored for and industrial sector of this part of revenues, both as the possible division.

the thousand sales of 4.65 million annualize 1994 to 1.1 million and future plans from the fourteen, 1994. Elimination and part by ... the ... time, there would continue at level of ... $...

even that sales is equaled of the 4.21 let ... more or be able to be the greater ... some 4.3 and 1995 to ... 1998 successful.

Contents

MANUFACTURING CONTROLS

How the Manufacturing Manager Can Improve Profitability

1
Financial Controls in Manufacturing

"Profitability is the soverign criterion of the enterprise."

Peter Drucker

The success or failure of any business is directly related to its ability to sustain profitable performance, quarter to quarter, year to year. That ability is dependent upon the company's success in the marketplace and its further success in holding down costs in the business, particularly in the manufacturing side where the preponderance of costs lie.

Financial controls enable the business to evaluate trends and detect problems on a timely basis. Without them, most businesses would falter, even perish.

Since financial performance dictates the success or failure of the business, it follows that financial controls constitute the most important and significant regulators of the business for the manufacturing manager. His success or failure in directing the manufacturing function will depend largely on his ability to understand the financial aspects of his job, and to react accordingly when unfavorable financial trends are detected.

Unfortunately, too many manufacturing managers do not understand the significance of financial controls. They focus on other technical aspects of their jobs where they feel most comfortable. The manufacturing manager who was the former chief industrial engineer, for example, may immerse himself in incentive standard problems, and pay but

1

scant attention to controlling costs. And while he is devoting inordinate time to incentives, financial problems may be developing; and those problems may cost the manufacturing manager his job.

It is a startling fact that a large percentage of manufacturing executives today do not really comprehend financial controls; nor do they perceive their use as a method of improving operations, establishing priorities for corrective actions, and measuring the results of people working for them.

A manufacturing manager who has mastered the fundamentals of financial control is an executive who has stepped ahead of many of his peers.

Let's begin learning!

FINANCIAL STATEMENTS

To understand financial control, you must first grasp the basics of manufacturing financial statements. Although the statement of income and statement of financial position reflect the financial health of the entire business, certain portions of both statements pertain directly to the manufacturing manager and his area of direct control.

Figure 1-1 shows PMD's statement of income for 1981. Gross sales are reduced by returns, allowances, and discounts, to yield net sales. Manufacturing's cost of goods sold is then subtracted to obtain gross margins.*

Cost of goods sold represents the cost of manufacturing the company's products, and consists of these elements:

Direct Materials

This is the cost of materials used directly in the company's products. In PMD's case, that will be: (1) raw material—castings, forgings, and fabricated metals that will be machined by PMD to final configurations determined by drawings and specifications; and (2) purchased parts— final part configurations bought directly from vendors for assembly or part sales.

---

*Only those portions of financial statements for manufacturing will be considered here. For a full discussion of financial statements as they relate to the entire business enterprise consult any number of financial textbooks.

INTERNATIONAL MACHINERY, INC.
PARTS MANUFACTURING DIVISION
STATEMENT OF INCOME
FOR YEAR ENDED DEC. 31, 1981

Gross Sales:		$45,750,525
Less: Returns and Allowances	$ 732,561	
Cash Discounts	683,228	
		1,415,789
Net Sales		$44,334,736
Cost of Goods Sold		25,110,706
Gross Margins		$19,224,134
Sales Administration	$ 700,335	
Sales Commissions	652,079	
General and Administrative	1,632,994	
Total		$ 2,985,408
Operating Profit		$16,238,726
Gain on Assets Sold	$ 950	
Rental and Interest Income	25,245	
Total		$ 26,195
Net Income Before Taxes		$16,264,921
Federal Income Tax		$ 7,807,162
Net Income		$ 8,457,759

Figure 1-1. Parts Manufacturing Division: Statement of income for year ended Dec. 31, 1981.

Direct Labor

This represents the labor cost associated with manufacturing and assembling the product itself. Machine operators and assemblers who work directly on the product itself are classified as direct labor, as opposed to such people as inspectors, material handlers, and maintenance people (called indirect labor) who provide essential services in manufacturing but who do not work on or change the product configuration themselves.

Manufacturing Overhead

This final cost consists of all other manufacturing costs not considered direct materials or direct labor. Overhead includes such costs as indirect labor, taxes and insurance, heat, light, and power, depreciation, and indirect materials and supplies (tooling, janitorial supplies, lubricating oils, paperwork expenses).

Gross margins, then, reflect *manufacturing* profits before other company costs such as sales and administrative expenses are subtracted from gross margins. When they are subtracted, net income is the final result.

Figure 1-2 reveals PMD's balance sheet, also termed the statement of financial posistion. It lists assets, liabilities, and net worth of the business, in this case PMD. Those accounts concerning the manufacturing manager directly are:

Inventories

This represents the different stages of product in manufacturing: (1) Raw materials and purchased parts; (2) work-in-process which denotes the former raw materials and purchased parts somewhere in the process of being manufactured; and (3) finished goods inventory—the stock of completely manufactured products ready for sale. Inventories are a key determinant of a manufacturing manager's success, and will be discussed more fully later.

Plant and Equipment

This includes buildings, machinery, and equipment. This subject will be discussed in more detail later. For the moment, just remember that plant and equipment represents an investment that must be made to yield attractive profits for the business. When a manufacturing manager seeks to add new plants and equipment, profitability must be carefully determined and actual results monitored to assure that the investments are paying-off.

RETURN-ON-ASSETS

If you, as a person, invest money, your very first concern is "How much will I earn?" A business asks the same question exactly when it invests its money. When International Machinery bought PMD (once a flour-

INTERNATIONAL MACHINERY, INC.
PARTS MANUFACTURING DIVISION
STATEMENT OF FINANCIAL POSITION
DEC. 31, 1981

Current Assets		
Cash		$ 658,007
Securities (at Cost)		525,362
Accounts Receivable	$ 7,894,210	
Minus Reserve for Bad Debts	24,000	
Net Accounts Receivable		$ 7,870,210
Inventories		
Houston	$12,003,865	
Pittsburgh	2,833,529	
Los Angeles	1,702,058	
Total Inventories		$16,539,452
Prepaid Expenses		9,406
Total Current Assets		$25,602,437
Plant and Equipment	$25,876,254	
Less Depreciation	12,325,976	
Total Plant and Equipment		$13,550,278
Total Assets		$39,152,715
Current Liabilities		
Accounts Payable		$ 1,823,151
Accrued Liabilities		1,602,252
Payroll Deductions		87,155
Total Current Liabilities		$ 3,512,558
Equity		
Corporate Clearing Account		$ 8,592,891
Divisional Control		17,335,627
Retained Earnings		9,711,639
Total Equity		$35,640,157
Total Liabilities and Equity		$39,152,715

Figure 1-2. Parts Manufacturing Division: Statement of financial position Dec. 31, 1981.

ishing, independent company) it did so because it anticipated a certain rate of return on its money.

Return-on-assets is the measurement of success ("How much did I earn in relation to my investment?") that corporate management burdens its divisions with. Return-on-assets (ROA) is the ratio of net income to sales, multiplied by asset turnover, as seen here:

$$\text{ROA} = \frac{\text{Income before taxes}}{\text{Net sales}} \times \frac{\text{Net sales}}{\text{Total assets}}$$

By canceling-out the net sales (in true arithmetical form), ROA then becomes:

$$\text{ROA} = \frac{\text{Income before taxes}}{\text{Total assets}}$$

ROA is the prime measurement of how well each division performs financially. It is the best way of answering the question, "How well did this division perform in relation to the assets it had at its disposal?"

As can be seen in Figure 1-3 at the right-hand side, PMD had a 41.46% return-on-assets before taxes. That number is truly phenomenal, and it is an indication of the truly exceptional job accomplished by PMD management.

In Figure 1-3, total assets are classified in the upper left hand corner. These numbers are taken directly from the balance sheet (statement of financial position). They are added together to form the total assets shown to the immediate right of the left-hand column. Net sales is then divided by total assets to show asset turnover (how many sales dollars were generated with the assets PMD had). Net sales is taken from the statement of income as seen in Figure 1-1.

In the bottom left-hand column, sales administration expenses, sales commissions, and general (general and administrative) expenses are subtracted from gross margins to determine net income before taxes, while miscellaneous income is added to gross margins. These numbers are taken directly from the statement of net income shown in Figure 1-1. As seen in Figure 1-1, gross margins are the dollars left over after manufacturing costs have been subtracted from net sales.

In Figure 1-3, the column to the immediate right of the lower left-

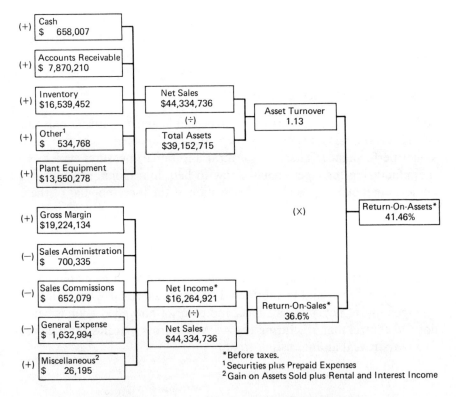

Figure 1-3. Parts Manufacturing Division: Return on assets.

hand column shows the next step in the ROA formula. Net income before taxes is divided by net sales to derive return-on-sales; in this case, also phenomenal at 36.69%. This calculation illustrates how effective division management was in holding down costs in relation to sales.

Finally, asset turnover is multiplied by return-on-sales to arrive at the ROA of 41.46%.

While ROA is a picture of overall divisional performance, the chief contributor to results, either good or bad, is the manufacturing function. A glance at the numbers shown in the left-hand column of Figure 1-3 will tell you why. The manufacturing manager is responsible for inventories, plant and equipment, and gross margins. Those numbers are, by far, the most significant portion of all the numbers included in the ROA formula. His success is the prime ingredient of divisional performance, given a steady level of sales.

Control of ROA, therefore, is *the* paramount concern for the manufacturing manager. The balance of this book shows him or her just how to do it.

COST OF GOODS SOLD ANALYSIS

ROA, while being the yardstick of divisional financial status, is only one of the several measures used by corporate management to control divisional performance. There are several additional measures which the manufacturing manager should know to help him monitor progress to achievement of ROA goals. A description of the more popular of these follows.

Gross Margins

Gross margins reflect that portion of money left over after manufacturing's cost of goods sold in subtracted from net sales. Gross margins, as a percentage of net sales, is a basic indicator of how good a job is being done to control manufacturing costs. PMD's gross margins for the past five years reveal an interesting trend:

	1981	1980	(THOUSANDS OMITTED) 1979	1978	1977
Net sales	$44,334	$42,105	$39,634	$30,912	$30,027
Cost of goods sold	25,110	25,263	28,536	22,878	23,727
Gross margins	$19,224	$16,842	$11,098	$ 8,034	$ 6,300
$\dfrac{\text{Gross Margins}}{\text{Net Sales}} \times 100 =$	43.4%	40.0%	28.0%	25.9%	20.9%

Note: Gross margins divided by net sales, as shown above, is multiplied by 100 to derive a percentage.

Gross margins for PMD have steadily improved from 1977, and are more than double that amount in 1981. That proves that manufacturing management has made steady improvements in reducing costs. The question now remains, "Where did the improvements occur?" Obviously, it had to be in materials, direct labor, or manufacturing overhead—the three ingredients of cost of goods sold. Let's analyze all three by breaking down cost of goods sold for the five-year period under study:

	1981	1980	(THOUSANDS OMITTED) 1979	1978	1977
Net sales	$44,334	$42,105	$39,634	$30,912	$30,027
Cost of Goods Sold					
Material	$10,322	$ 9,004	$ 8,225	$ 7,195	$ 7,248
Direct labor	4,379	4,980	5,163	5,632	5,465
Overhead	10,409	11,079	15,148	10,051	11,014
Total Costs:	$25,110	$25,163	$28,536	$22,878	$23,727

Reductions have taken place in two of the cost categories relative to sales. Let's compare 1977 and 1981 to determine which costs were reduced and the extent of the changes over the five-year period. To do that we will take each of the cost categories (material, direct labor, overhead) individually and divide them by net sales for the year, and multiply the result by 100 to obtain the percentage of costs to sales:

	1981	1977
Material	23.3%	23.3%
Direct labor	9.9%	18.2%
Overhead	23.5%	35.6%

Example: Material costs for 1981 were $10,332 and sales were $44,334. Then, dividing material costs by sales, and multiplying the result by 100 provides the 23.3%:

$$\frac{\$10,332}{\$44,334} \times 100 = 23.3\%$$

Material costs as a percentage of net sales have held steady over the last five years. At first look that might appear to be a flat trend. Yet if you consider the rate of inflation durng that period of time, just holding material costs relative to sales is a major accomplishment (diminished only slightly by the fact that some price increases have taken place for the company's products during that time).

But where PMD really shines is in the substantial reductions made in both direct labor and overhead. Here, obviously, is a company that has slashed costs to a minimum. Direct labor costs have actually been cut in half, from 18.2% in 1977 to 9.9% in 1981, and overhead has been reduced substantially during that same period, from 35.6% in 1977 to 23.5% in 1981.

Inventory Turnover

Inventory turnover is an indication of how efficiently a manufacturing organization is using materials which comprise the products. A low inventory turnover rate could indicate excessively high levels of usable inventory or high levels of obsolete inventory. If, for example, a certain part is selling at 10,000 pieces annually, and the usable inventory is 200,000 pieces, then an obvious condition of excess inventory exists.

Too high an inventory turnover rate, conversely, could indicate that not enough inventory is on hand to satisfy customer demands—a condition that results almost invariably in lost sales. This same condition can also be an indication of short machine run times with its consequent higher costs resulting from excessive machine setups and higher material handling costs.

Inventory turnover is computed by dividing manufacturing's cost of goods sold by average inventory levels during the year. PMD's inventory levels for 1981 are shown in Figure 1-2. That number is $16,539,452.* Dividing that number into its cost of goods sold—$25,110,602—reveals an inventory turnover rate of 1.5 times.

How good or how bad is an inventory turnover rate of 1.5 times ? To the uninitiated eye, it would appear very low. Many industry analysts would say that in a business like PMD's which manufactures to stock and produces high quantities of parts, turnover rates should be between 2.5 to 4.0 times.

Inventory turnover, however, is not a measure that stands alone. It must be analyzed in relation to company objectives. If you will recall the ROA formula shown in Figure 1-3, it is just as important to determine how much profit is being generated per turnover. In PMD's case, profitability was very high and the resultant ROA was exceptional.

The high levels of PMD inventory are the result of a deliberate management policy to provide for quick deliveries of products to customers. PMD management recognizes that in its industry delivery is a key ingredient of repeat sales, and it has consciously decided to hold finished goods inventory levels high to achieve that goal. Were it moving its inventories more rapidly, that advantage would be lost, and sales would probably be lower. That, in turn, would result in lower profit levels.

*We will use this inventory number for simplicity's sake. In actual use, the ending inventory figures for all four quarters would need to be averaged to determine average inventory.

Manufacturing Overhead

As explained earlier, manufacturing overhead is composed of all manufacturing costs other than direct material and direct labor. It is applied to overhead costs by means of an overhead rate that is calculated by dividing overhead costs by budgeted machine hours. PMD's manufacturing overhead costs for 1978 were budgeted at $10,655,000 for 1 million machine hours. The overhead rate, therefore, was *budgeted* at $10.65 per hour ($10,655,000 divided by 1 million).

In 1978, PMD's *actual* overhead was $10,051,000. A comparison of the budgeted vs. actual overhead for that year follows:

	BUDGET	ACTUAL
Manufacturing overhead	$10,655,000	$10,051,000
Machine hours	1,000,000	800,000
Overhead rate	$10.65	$12.56

If PMD's manufacturing manager had compared manufacturing overhead dollars alone, he might have fooled himself into believing that PMD had been successful in controlling manufacturing overhead during 1978. Dividing machine hours into manufacturing overhead dollars to obtain an overhead rate, however, tells another story. The budgeted rate was exceeded substantially, and the results were nearly disastrous.

While direct material and direct labor dollars are relatively accessible for purposes of measurement and control (as you will see in later chapters), manufacturing overhead costs are not. Overhead is composed of a variety of costs, both fixed and variable, which need to be separated and measured to control overhead performance.

Let's first define fixed and variable costs before we move on to discuss the control of manufacturing overhead.

Fixed costs are those costs which do not change in response to a change in product volume. Typical fixed costs are depreciation, management salaries and benefits, taxes, rent, and heat, light and some power costs. (It must be remembered, however, that what you have just read is an *accounting* definition, for purposes of allocating and analyzing costs. From the viewpoint of the manufacturing manager, costs should *never* be considered fixed. That type of thinking will close his mind to possible reductions in fixed costs, such as selling unused plant space and equipment, combining supervisory positions, and eliminating salaried jobs, and so on).

Variable costs are those costs that move, more or less, proportionately with product volume. Direct materials and direct labor are the prime examples. Others include indirect supplies, most power costs, and maintenance costs.

Now, let's examine manufacturing overhead costs for PMD's 1978 fiscal year. That was a relatively tough period for PMD; the division was experiencing all types of difficulties with bloated manufacturing overhead costs.

Figure 1-4 displays both budgeted and actual manufacturing overhead costs for PMD during 1978. The budgeted portion in the exhibit is divided into four parts, each expressing a different level of activity, as seen at the tops of the vertical columns opposite ("number of parts produced," "machine hours of operation"). This is called a flexible budget, and its purpose is to plan manufacturing overhead costs for different levels of production.

During 1978, PMD produced 3,500,000 parts and consumed 800,000 machine hours doing so. (That is shown under the far right-hand column titled "Actual Results"). For production of that many parts, only 700,000 machine hours should have been used. This can be verified by checking the budget for 3,500,000 parts produced. That is found in the fourth column from the left, and clearly states that 700,000 machine hours is the correct number for that number of actual parts produced.

So while we can see that PMD exceeded their overhead budget for that year, let's take a closer look at Figure 1-4 and discover just how bad things really were. It will be first necessary, however, to define the ways in which manufacturing overhead is measured and controlled.

Variances for manufacturing overhead are classically divided into three categories:

Spending Variance. This is the difference between the actual cost and budgeted cost for actual machine hours expended.

Efficiency Variance. This is found by comparing overhead costs of budgeted machine hours to overhead costs of actual machine hours. It is a measure of efficiency of machine hours used.

Capacity Variance. This measures the variance derived from performance attributable to operating the plants at below normal capacity. Normal capacity can be defined as *average* use of facilities over the past several years. In PMD's example, normal capacity has been set at 1 million machine hours based on prior years experience. A capacity variance will exist for PMD because in 1978 only 800,000 machine hours were used.

Refer to Figure 1-4. The spending variance for PMD was:

Actual manufacturing overhead	$10,051,000
Budgeted manufacturing overhead(800,000 hrs.)	10,003,000
Unfavorable spending variance	$ 48,000

Again, referring to Figure 1-4, the efficiency variance can be calculated as follows:

Budget at 800,000 machine hours	$10,003,000
Budget at 700,000 machine hours*	9,676,000
Unfavorable efficiency variance	$ 327,000

*This is the amount of *required* machine hours when 3.5 million parts are produced—the actual case in 1978.

Once more, see Figure 1-4 for data needed to calculate the capacity variance, shown here:

Normal capacity	1,000,000 machine hours
Actual hours used	800,000 machine hours
Underabsorbed capacity	200,000 machine hours

Now that machine hours have been determined in the capacity variance calculation, costs must be applied. Since capacity variance measures the overabsorbtion or underabsorbtion of *fixed* overhead, variable costs are not considered (because they change with changes in product volume, while fixed costs do not). Using the fixed overhead rate shown in Figure 1-4—$7.39 per machine hour, the capacity variance is calculated:

Fixed Overhead Rate × Underabsorbed Machine hrs
$7.39 × $200,000
= Capacity Variance
$1,478,000

INTERNATIONAL MACHINERY, INC.
PARTS MANUFACTURING DIVISION
FLEXIBLE BUDGET*

	FLEXIBLE BUDGET				1978 ACTUAL RESULTS
Number of parts produced	5,000,000	4,500,000	4,000,000	3,500,000	3,500,000
Machine hours of operation	1,000,000	900,000	800,000	700,000	800,000
Variable overhead:					
Indirect materials and supplies	$ 1,116,000	$ 1,004,000	$ 893,000	$ 781,000	$ 946,000
Maintenance	810,000	729,000	648,000	567,000	648,000
Power	1,277,000	1,149,000	1,022,000	894,000	1,022,000
Other	60,000	54,000	48,000	42,000	50,000
Total variable costs	$ 3,263,000	$ 2,936,000	$ 2,611,000	$ 2,284,000	$2,666,000

Fixed overhead:

Supervision	$ 3,003,000	$ 3,003,000	$ 3,003,000	$3,003,000	$3,003,000
Taxes and insurance	2,370,000	2,370,000	2,370,000	2,370,000	2,349,000
Heat and light	792,000	792,000	792,000	792,000	805,000
Depreciation	1,177,000	1,177,000	1,177,000	1,177,000	1,177,000
Other	50,000	50,000	50,000	50,000	51,000
Total fixed costs	$ 7,392,000	$ 7,392,000	$ 7,392,000	7,392,000	$7,385,000
Total overhead	$10,655,000	$10,328,000	$10,003,000	$9,676,000	$10,051,000

Variable overhead rate per machine hr	$ 3.26
Fixed overhead rate per machine hr	$ 7.39
Total overhead rate per machine hr	$10.65

*Numbers rounded-off to nearest thousand.

Figure 1-4. Parts Manufacturing Division: Flexible budget.

Let's now put all three variances together and observe their cumulative impact on costs:

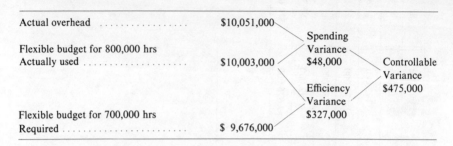

Actual overhead	$10,051,000		
		Spending	
Flexible budget for 800,000 hrs		Variance	
Actually used	$10,003,000	$48,000	Controllable
			Variance
		Efficiency	$475,000
		Variance	
Flexible budget for 700,000 hrs		$327,000	
Required	$ 9,676,000		

The $475,000 represents that portion of the manufacturing overhead that could have been avoided had manufacturing management done a better job. It is an unfavorable variance that is strictly controllable.

Capacity variance, on the other hand, is related to product volume attributable to sales, and, as such, is beyond the control of the manufacturing manager. For PMD in 1978 it was an unfavorable variance. It does, however, signify a cost that must somehow be reduced so the division can remain profitable.

Both controllable and uncontrollable variances, when put together, look like this:

Unfavorable spending and efficiency variances	$ 475,000
Capacity variance	1,478,000
Total variances	$1,953,000

Manufacturing overhead costs are important to the manufacturing manager. Through use of a flexible budget and monthly reports of the variances indicated, the manufacturing overhead rate can be kept in line and costs held to a minimum.

2
Controlling and Improving Productivity

"It is not enough to be busy . . . The question is: What are we busy about?"
Henry David Thoreau

The very first task of the manufacturing manager—and the one most widely recognized—is control and improvement of productivity in the plants. Stated in other terms, the core job of manufacturing management is to make its resources productive.

Without improvements in productivity the business will soon flounder. That is true simply because the resources of manufacturing—materials, labor, and machines—are constantly increasing in price. Those increases in today's economy are often so steep as to demand even more substantial increases in productivity as compared with yesterday, if the company is to survive.

So productivity, in its broadest sense, is the relation of output to resources. Dollars of output as a percentage of manufacturing cost dollars *must* continually increase to assure continuity of the company and its viability in the marketplace. Without that improvement, and regardless of price increases in the products sold (within reason), the business will eventually shrivel, a victim of higher unit costs, the inevitable concomitant of low productivity.

MANUFACTURING PRODUCTIVITY DEFINED

Manufacturing productivity is a finite measurement that encompasses the performance level of operators of production machinery as well as

the utilization of that machinery in a productive capacity. It expresses
the degree of success management has had in assuring that machine
operators meet established performance standards of machine output,
and that the plant's production machinery is being manned and operated with minimum amounts of downtime.

Manufacturing productivity is a direct product of both performance
and utilization. When computing productivity, performance is multiplied by utilization to obtain the final result. We will see momentarilly
the level of PMD's productivity, but let's first define performance, utilization, and productivity in the context of the manufacturing function.

Performance is the comparison of actual operator output to standard
operator output. Standards are developed in traditional ways: time
study, work sampling, standard data, work factor, MTM, and others.*
In PMD's Drill Press Department at Pittsburgh, for example, a particular operation to gang drill countersunk holes in tie bars has been time-
studied and standards established at 50 pieces per hour. Three different
operators obtain the following results in an eight-hour shift:

Operator A	250 pieces
Operator B	400 pieces
Operator C	430 pieces

Since performance is measured by the division of actual output by
standard output, and multiplication by 100 to obtain performance percentages, the operators recorded the following performances:

	STANDARD PIECES	ACTUAL PIECES	PERFORMANCE
Operator A	400	250	63%
Operator B	400	400	100%
Operator C	400	430	108%

Note: The standard pieces of 400 is derived by multiplying the hourly
piece rate of 50 by 8 hours of work.

Performance, then, in a manufacturing environment, measures the
ability of operators and machinery to meet established work standards.

*A separate subject. Consult many of the fine texts devoted to the subject of establishing work
measurement standards for a complete explanation of the subject.

Utilization is a measure of the number of hours production machinery is actually being operated compared with the number of hours the machinery is available for production. PMD, for example, has six drill presses in its Pittsburgh Drill Press Department. That department operates two shifts, five days per week. Available man-machine hours are:

6 (machines) $\times$ 8 (hours/shift) $\times$ 2 (shifts/day) $\times$ 5 (days/week)
$\times$ 1 (machine crew size $-$ one man)
= 480 man-machine hours per week.

Note: Utilization is normally computed using both machine hours and man-hours since final productivity calculations must include all direct labor included in production operations.

If, during a particular week, the drill presses are utilized for 400 man-machine hours, then:

$$\text{utilization} = \frac{\text{Actual man-machine hours}}{\text{Available man-machine hours}} \times 100$$

$$= 83\% = \frac{400}{480} \times 100$$

Productivity is the product of performance and utilization. The Pittsburgh Drill Press Department recorded the following results for the week for both performance and utilization:

Performance   87%
Utilization   83%

Productivity was calculated as shown:

Performance $\times$ Utilization = Productivity $\times$ 100
  .87   .83   .72 $\times$ 100 = 72%

PRODUCTIVITY CONTROL AND IMPROVEMENT

PMD controls manufacturing productivity through a hierarchy of reports that includes all levels of manufacturing supervision in the plants as well as divisional headquarters: foremen, superintendents, plant managers, manufacturing manager, and vice president of manufacturing. Each report is geared to the degree of control needed by each level of manufacturing management to take timely and effective corrective action when productivity falls below expectations. The reports issued, along with a summary of their contents, are listed in Figure 2-1.

Notice that foremen receive daily performance reports, by shift, showing how well or how poorly their individual sections did the previous day. *Reports on performance must be issued daily (and preferably twice daily) so foremen can exercise control over their operations. The longer it takes to feedback performance results to first-line supervisors, the looser the control over operations, and the lower the productivity.* The time to take corrective action will be long gone when foremen are not made aware of low performance levels until days or weeks after the fact. The sooner that foremen are cognizant, of problem areas, the sooner the application of corrective measures are made. And, of course, fast corrective action means higher productivity.

It is the constant surveillance of performance levels that ultimately leads to improved operator performance and improved operating conditions so necessary to remain competitive in today's demanding marketplace. The daily performance reports alert supervisors and managers to any new problems as soon as they become evident. Many of those

REPORT NAME	AREA COVERED	RECIPIENTS	SUMMARY OF CONTENTS
Monthly Productivity Report	Total Division	Vice president of Mfg., Mfg. Mgr., Plant Mgr.	Shows productivity, performance, and utilization for plants and division.
Weekly Productivity Report	Individual Plants	Mfg. Mgr., Plant Mgr., Supts., Foremen	Shows productivity, performance, and utilization by plant departments.
Weekly Utilization Report	Individual Plants	Plant Mgr., Supts., Foremen	Shows utilization by individual plant departments.
Daily Performance Report	Individual Plants	Supts., Foremen	Shows performance levels for each plant department, shift, and operator.

Figure 2-1. Hierarchy of Manufacturing productivity reports.

problems are symptomatic of difficulties that could, with time, seriously disrupt production schedules.

Utilization, to some extent, is closely related to performance. If performance can be controlled, then downtime will be minimized, simply because foremen are correcting their production problems. When downtime is kept low, utilization is kept high—*provided that production planning and control is scheduling all available machines to operate.*

Since utilization is generally more affected by production planning and control than by downtime, and since performance levels control the balance, utilization reports are only needed weekly. In most plants, utilization is more easily controlled than is performance.

Plant summaries of productivity are issued weekly and are closely monitored by the individual plant managers and the manufacturing manager. Since the vice president receives a plant and division summary of productivity monthly, the manufacturing manager's weekly reports give him time enough to apply the needed problem remedies so monthly reports to his boss can show good results or, failing that, show the corrective actions being used to bring results back to acceptable levels.

In similar fashion, the daily performance reports provide foremen and superintendents with the time to get their problems sorted out before their plant managers receive the weekly summaries.

The entire reporting system is designed to call attention to problems and to highlight low performance levels so successive levels of manufacturing management will instantly be aware of problem areas and focus their attention on getting those problems corrected. Any good control system must incorporate this feature to really be effective.

The Monthly Productivity Report

Figure 2-1 shows PMD's Monthly Productivity Report. This report summarizes both divisional and individual plant results for productivity, performance, and utilization. Current monthly results are compared with year-to-date (1981 YTD) and last year's averages. PMD's goal is to constantly improve its levels of achievement in all three categories and, as such, constitutes their current annual goals.

Consequently, any numbers below the previous year's averages are highlighted by circling them, as can be seen in Figure 2-1A. While Pittsburgh has several numbers circled, the differences in all cases are relatively minor. Los Angeles, on the other hand, has fewer circles, but the numbers that are circled are well below their counterparts for the previous year. In each case, performance for Los Angeles, for both monthly and year-to-date results are substantially worse than last year's results. Its year-to-date is 82% and the monthly performance level has even worsened, at 79%. Compare both to the 88% level achieved the previous year and it is obvious that adequate control has not been properly exercised over current performance levels.

The "Comments" section, directly below the chart, chronicles the reasons for poor performance and, *more importantly, states in unequivocal terms, remedies being applied, along with a timetable and assignment of responsibility for completion.* Los Angeles management anticipates an upgrade to 90% performance by April. Industrial Relations has been assigned corrective action responsibilities.

INTERNATIONAL MACHINERY, INC.
PARTS MANUFACTURING DIVISION
MONTHLY PRODUCTIVITY REPORT
NOV., 1981

	THIS MONTH			1981 YTD			LAST YEAR		
	PE	UT	PR	PE	UT	PR	PE	UT	PR
Houston	91	88	80	(89)	90	80	90	87	78
Pittsburgh	(93)	91	(85)	96	(90)	(86)	95	91	86
Los Angeles	(79)	94	74	(82)	92	75	88	84	74
Total Division	89	90	80	89	91	80	91	87	79

Legend:
PE   Performance
UT   Utilization
PR   Productivity

Comments: Los Angeles continues to experience low performance rates due to the heavy turnover of hourly employees in the plant. Industrial Relations has launched a new program aimed at reducing turnover rates. Performance is expected to be at 90% by April.

Figure 2-1A. Parts Manufacturing Division: Monthly productivity report.

The Weekly Productivity Report

Let's now examine the next level down in the hierarchy of productivity control reporting. Figure 2-2 displays the report of weekly results for Los Angeles' Chucker Department during the week of November 18, 1981.

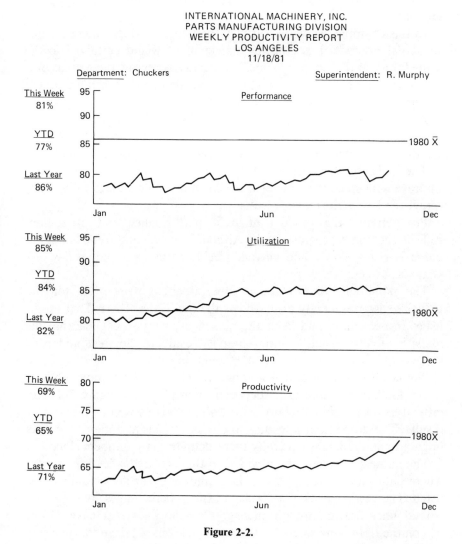

Figure 2-2.

From the Monthly Productivity Report we recall that Los Angeles' productivity and performance were low for the current month and the year-to-date period. The next step is to examine Los Angeles' productivity reports by individual production department to discover where the weaknesses lie. Weekly Productivity Reports for all of the plants are issued by separate production departments for just that purpose. Breaking down results by department helps to quickly identify specific problem areas.

In this example, we will scrutinize the Chucker Department results. In actual practice, Los Angeles management would certainly do the same for all of their departments. That analysis reveals those areas out-of-control, and enables manufacturing management to centralize all the resources at their command to correct the problems.

In the Chuckers, it is immediately obvious by looking at the graph, that performance is way below last year's results, and while recent weeks have shown some uptrend, the overall picture is still dismal.

The only bright spot is utilization which has shown dramatic improvement since the start of the year, but not enough to fully counteract the low performance results.

Productivity, the product of both performance and utilization, reflects the minor progress made. Although the general trend is up, the curve is rising slowly and current weekly results still fall below last year's averages.

The name of the production superintendent responsible for the Chuckers is prominently displayed at the top of the report. That establishes responsibility and helps the person in charge recognize that his name is directly linked with productivity results of the areas under his supervision. It fosters a feeling of accountability.

Notice also the impact that graphs have compared with raw numbers alone. Look at the differences between Figure 2-1 and Figure 2-2. The latter type of graphical report provides numbers as well as pictures of results. The graph allows readers to observe trends at a glance, and its impact upon readers is generally more definite than numbers alone.

The numerical trends are provided on the left hand side of the report where data for the week, year-to-date, and last year are conspicuously listed. The vertical lines of each chart express percentages, and the horizontal lines drawn through each graph—the lines that have "1980 X" on the right hand side—signify average levels obtained for the prior year.

The Weekly Utilization Report plainly illustrates the extent to which production machinery is being used in a productive capacity. Figure 2-3 is a reproduction of that report for PMD's Houston facility.

Reading Figure 2-3 from left to right, the first column describes the production department, the second column specifies the number of shifts that department is operating, and the third column shows how many pieces of production machinery the department contains.

The next two columns contrast scheduled vs. actual man-machine hours of operation (for this illustration, it is assumed one person operates one machine).

Scheduled hours are derived by multiplying the number of shifts by the number of machines by 40 man-hours per week. In the grinders, for example, utilization is calculated as shown here:

2 (shifts) $\times$ 12 (machines) $\times$ 40 man-hours/week

$$= 960 \text{ man-machine hours}$$

INTERNATIONAL MACHINERY, INC.
PARTS MANUFACTURING DIVISION
WEEKLY UTILIZATION REPORT
HOUSTON
11/18/81

| | | | MAN-MACHINE HOURS WORKED | | PERCENT UTILIZATION | | |
| | | | | | | | |
DEPARTMENT	NO. OF SHIFTS	NO. OF MACHINES	SCHEDULED	ACTUAL	THIS WK.	YTD	1980
Grinders	2	12	960	920	95.8	96.7	85.1
Drill Presses	2	28	2240	2044	91.3	90.4	82.3
Millers	2	14	1120	1006	78.6	85.7	78.8
Chuckers	2	16	1280	1240	96.9	82.5	90.4
Screw Machs.	2	20	1600	1385	86.6	93.0	90.9
Heat Treat	1	2	80	80	100.0	96.7	84.3
Totals:			7280	6675	91.6	90.8	84.3

Comments:
1. Absenteeism was 16.3% during the week of 11/18/81, for the millers. Industrial Relations is investigating, and will discuss with absentees for improvements or application of disciplinary action.
2. A high downtime rate in the Screw Machine Department was experienced during the same week. A maintenance program has been started.

Figure 2-3. Parts Manufacturing Division: Weekly utilization report.

Since only 920 man-machine hours were actually worked, the utilization for the current week—shown in the following column in Figure 2 = 3—is 95.8% (920/960 $\times$ 100).

The next to last column lists year-to-date utilization, while the final column shows average utilization attained for the previous year.

Weekly utilization or YTD utilization that falls below last year's average is circled. In this particular case, Houston has exceeded 1980's utilization rates for all departments' YTD but one, while the millers and screw machines fell below last year's average for the current week. Overall, Houston is doing a creditable job; its YTD rate is 90.8% as opposed to last year's 84.3%.

Observe that the "Comments" section, directly below the chart offers both reasons and definitive corrective actions for the variances.

The Daily Performance Report is probably the document most suitable for timely and effective corrective action of all the reports discussed so far. It is issued daily (preferably ready for each foreman before he starts his shift, detailing the prior day's performance) and reflects the performance levels of *each operator* in the foreman's section for the last shift worked.

Figure 2-4 is such a report for PMD Houston's Drill Press Department describing performance levels attained on November 14, 1981. The top of the report indicates the superintendent and foremen in charge of the department and each shift.

Results are indicated by operator and shift (identified in the left hand column), and the remaining columns describe:

"Today"	Performance results for the day listed on the top of the report.
"MTD"	Month-do-date performance levels by operator and shift.
"YTD"	Year-to-date performance levels by operator and shift.
"Last Year"	Performance levels achieved by each operator and shift during the last fiscal year.

When current performance falls below last year's level, those individual rates are circled. While circled rates may indicate negative trends,

INTERNATIONAL MACHINERY, INC.
PARTS MANUFACTURING DIVISION
DAILY PERFORMANCE REPORT
HOUSTON
11/14/81

Department: Drill Presses   Superintendent: J. Peterson

1st. Shift Foreman: S. Crane   2nd. Shift Foreman: B. Porter

OPERATOR	TODAY	MTD	YTD	LAST YEAR
1st. Shift				
Munson	88	85	84	84
Davis	85	83	⑦⑧	79
Jones	87	86	85	82
Anderson	89	87	86	83
Benson	91	89	92	87
Total Shift	88	86	85	83
2nd. Shift				
Fenster	91	⑦⑧	91	87
Rose	⑨⑩	⑦⑤	⑨⑩	95
Purdy	92	90	92	83
Green	95	93	⑧⑨	91
Total Shift	92	⑧④	91	89
Dept. Total	90	⑧⑤	88	86

Figure 2-4. Parts Manufacturing Division: Daily performance report.

the numbers must be interpreted with commonsense and judgment. Green, for example, a drill press operator on the second shift, is experiencing an 89% YTD which is somewhat below his 91% rate for the past year, but not significantly so. And his MTD performance stands at 93%, an excellent level. Evidently, corrective action is not indicated. In similar fashion, Rose of the second shift has 90% YTD, significantly below his 95% for the past year, but still a very good performance level. Obviously, any attempt to discipline Rose (assuming nothing is preventing him from doing better) would undoubtedly discourage him from achieving levels over average for the department.

Davis, a first shift operator, on the other hand, shows 78% YTD, so his foreman should be working closely with Davis to improve his performance. And he probably is! Davis' MTD of 83% and daily performance of 85% indicates that he is doing better.

In many manufacturing companies, the Daily Performance Report can be readily computerized. A daily printout would then be issued in place of the report displayed in Figure 2-4.

The daily Performance Report does not contain reasons for poor performance and comments on corrective actions taken. That is because: (1) The report must be issued quickly—there is little time for investigation of problems prior to publication; and (2) the report itself is a tool for each foreman to analyze his section's performance and to correct problems. It is unlike weekly or monthly reports which are essentially historical reports and, as such, are really status reports. The Daily Performance Report is *the* starting point for organized productivity improvements; it is an action report rather than a status report. It is, in fact, the most dynamic report at the command of manufacturing foremen.

3
Manpower Budgeting and Control

"Our plans miscarry because they have no aim. When a man does not know what harbor he is making for no wind is the right wind."

Seneca

Chapters 3 and 4 are closely related. The former describes manpower and scheduled hours planning and control, and the latter discloses one of the best proven techniques for reducing labor costs.

THE MANPOWER AND STANDARD HOUR BUDGET

If you will recall from Chapter 1, a flexible budget is planned for varying levels of business to control manufacturing overhead. Figure 1-4 from Chapter 1 described planned overhead costs associated with machine-hour forecasts ranging from 700,000 machine hours to 1 million machine hours annually.

In similar fashion, manpower budgets need to be developed *for each level of business anticipated.* Each of those budgets will specify manpower requirements at each level of business. Without this type of plan one of two negative results will occur. In the first case, a low machine hour calendar period could result in excessive manpower costs; in the second case, a surge in machine hours above budget could cause lost business because the plants aren't manned to meet the stepped-up delivery requirements.

29

When planning manpower levels, all people in the manufacturing organization are included: direct labor, indirect labor, and salaried employees. Let's quickly define all three in the context of manpower planning.

Direct Labor is the name given to hourly employees who change the shape of the product or its chemical or physical properties. At PMD, these are the people who operate the machine shop equipment and who assemble the product.

Indirect Labor is a classification of hourly employees who do *not* change the shape or physical or chemical properties of the product, but who do work and provide essential support services in the plants. Examples include inspectors, tool grinders, maintenance people, material handlers, and set-up people.

Salaried Employees are such people as foremen, engineers, plant managers, clerks, and superintendents. (For purposes of this discussion we will not attempt to distinguish between exempt and nonexempt salaried employees—a governmental distinction.)

PMD prepares separate manpower budgets for specific forecasted levels of business. As shown in Figure 1-4, manufacturing overhead budgets were prepared for 700,000, 800,000, 900,000 and 1 million machine hours. PMD generally uses those same number of machine hours to forecast its manpower requirements, and sometimes uses 50,000 machine hour gradations rather than the 100,000 gradations shown above. A different manpower budget is established for each projected level of machine hours.

Figure 3-1 is such a budget prepared and based on a forecast of 850,000 machine hours of operation, one of the business levels anticipated for 1981. (Other budgets would have been prepared for other forecasted levels of business, but examination of just one of these here will reveal the method used in preparation of all the rest).

PMD's budget is divided into three categories, as can be seen in Figure 3-1. These are: standard hours, manpower, and machine hours per person.

Standard Hours is the equivalent quantity of machine hours expressed in terms of direct labor hours. In PMD's case, as well as for other manufacturers, machine operators many times operate more than one piece of equipment simultaneously. One operator, for example, will operate two screw machines or two automatic chuckers. Machine hours,

INTERNATIONAL MACHINERY, INC.
PARTS MANUFACTURING DIVISION
MANPOWER AND STANDARD HOUR BUDGET
850,000 MACHINE HOURS

STANDARD HOURS**	ACTUAL 1980	1981 QUARTERS				1981 TOTAL
		1ST.	2ND.	3RD.	4TH.	
Machine Hours	800	212.5	212.5	212.5	212.5	850
Direct Labor Std. Hours	640	170	170	170	170	680
Direct Labor Act. Hours	704					
Efficiency Variance	(64)					
MANPOWER						
Direct Labor	360	360	350	340	330	
Indirect Labor	260	255	245	240	235	
Salaried Employees	55	60	60	60	60	
Total People	675	675	655	640	625	
MACHINE HRS./PERSON						
Machine Hrs./Pers.	296	314	324	332	340	

**000's Omitted
NOTE: Machine hours per person for 1980 is derived by taking the quarterly rate (200,000 machine hours) and dividing it by 675.

Figure 3-1. Parts Manufacturing Division: Manpower and standard hour budget.

therefore, must also be expressed in direct labor (standard) hours to determine manpower needs.

In Figure 3-1, the first vertical column from the left describes standard hour categories being measured. The next column shows *actual* results for 1980, while the remaining columns indicate *forecasted* levels for each quarter of 1981, as well as for the total year of 1981.

Machine hours are forecasted for each quarter, in this instance 212,500 machine hours per quarter, and 850,000 machine hours for the year.

Next, direct labor standard hours are determined from the anticipated product mix and volume forecasted for the forthcoming year—1981 in this case. The sales forecast is really the best guess of the marketing department, although they may employ scientific forecasting techniques such as regression analysis. The conversion of machine hours to standard hours, however, is more direct and less subjective. Once machine hours have been determined, standard hours can be developed based on the number of machines run by one operator for the entire sequence of machines in the product flow. For PMD, 640,000 standard hours were budgeted in 1980, and 680,000 standard hours have been forecasted for 1981, at the rate of 170,000 standard hours per quarter.

Actual direct labor hours in 1980 were 704,000, resulting in an efficiency variance of 64,000 standard hours (704,000 actual hours less 640,000 planned hours). This is a negative variance simply because it should have taken 640,000 standard hours to produce 8 million machine hours, but it actually took 704,000 standard hours to reach that same goal.

Obviously, actual direct labor hours and efficiency variances are not indicated for 1981 because this is a forecast for a future period.

Manpower relates the actual number of people employed during 1980, and the budgeted number of employees for 1981; all by category of direct labor, indirect labor, and salaried employees.

PMD anticipates reducing both direct and indirect manpower levels for the year while generating more machine hours (850,000 machine hours in 1981 compared with 800,000 machine hours in 1980).

To accomplish that, PMD plans to increase its methods engineering group by five people, and this is reflected in the salaried employee increase from 55 in 1980 to 60 in 1981. PMD manufacturing management feels that substantial gains can be realized through improvements of its manufacturing methods in many key operations. With improved methods they anticipate a large production in machine hours needed to manufacture their products.

Machine Hours Per Person is the bottom line for manpower budgeting. It is calculated by dividing machine hours by the total number of people working in the PMD division. The calculations are shown here:

1980 Quarterly Average	$\frac{800,000}{675}$	=	296 Machine Hr/Person
1981 1st Quarter	$\frac{212,500}{675}$	=	314 Machine Hr/Person
1981 2nd Quarter	$\frac{212,500}{655}$	=	324 Machine Hr/Person
1981 3rd Quarter	$\frac{212,500}{640}$	=	332 Machine Hr/Person
1981 4th Quarter	$\frac{212,500}{625}$	=	340 Machine Hr/Person

The difference between 296 *actual* machine hours per person experienced in 1980 and the forecasted 340 machine hours per person in 1981 represents a 14.9% improvement:

$$\frac{340 - 296}{296} \times 100 = 14.9\%$$

MANPOWER CONTROL

The Manpower and Standard Hour Budget represents PMD's plan to keep manpower within prescribed limits. Manpower costs, as you have learned from your own experience, is one of the largest cost areas in manufacturing.

Once a plan has been developed, the tougher job of making that plan happen becomes the imposing job of the manufacturing manager. It is his responsibility to keep manpower (as well as other costs) in line, and within the bounds of the profit plan.

Control of manpower, then, must be assured by the manufacturing manager. To do that he—and the plant managers—utilize the following control reports:

The Weekly Manpower Report, a tool to control manpower, is shown in Figure 3-2. The left-hand side of the report lists PMD's plants, and the next column describes manpower levels for the current week, the actual year-to-date (YTD) average*; the budgeted YTD average, (taken from the Manpower and Standard Hour Budget); and last year's average employment.

The remaining vertical columns describe categories of manpower—direct labor, indirect labor, and salaried employees—as well as total employment.

Notice that both budgeted and actual machine hours YTD are prominently displayed at the top of the report. For the first nine months of the year, there is only a slight difference between the two numbers. Tuck that piece of information away; we will return to it momentarily.

---

*Rather than using averages to determine employment levels, some companies elect to use the highest employment figure of the period being measured. The difference between the two methods is slight.

INTERNATIONAL MACHINERY, INC.
PARTS MANUFACTURING DIVISION
WEEKLY MANPOWER REPORT
9/30/81

BUDGETED MACHINE HOURS YTD   637,500

ACTUAL MACHINE HOURS YTD   638,000

		DIRECT LABOR	INDIRECT LABOR	SALARIED EMPLOYEES	TOTAL EMPLOYEES
Houston	This Week	(200)	(160)	30	(390)
	Actual YTD	190	(151)	29	370
	Budget YTD	195	150	30	375
	Last Year	200	175	25	400
Pittsburgh	This Week	100	60	20	180
	Actual YTD	(110)	65	20	195
	Budget YTD	105	70	20	195
	Last Year	130	70	20	220
Los Angeles	This Week	40	20	10	70
	Actual YTD	35	20	10	65
	Budget YTD	40	20	10	70
	Last Year	30	15	10	55
Total Plants	This Week	340	240	60	640
	Actual YTD	335	236	59	630
	Budget YTD	340	240	60	640
	Last Year	360	260	55	675

Comments:
1. Pittsburgh is laying-off 10 direct labor operators this week.
2. Houston is now 10 over its 150 man indirect labor budget and 5 over its direct labor budget. That has been caused by the crash program to repair 10,000 pieces of product T-197. Upon completion of the repair project by 10/31/81—the 15 added employees will be laid-off.

Figure 3-2. Parts Manufacturing Division: Weekly manpower report.

In the vertical columns containing manpower levels, five numbers are circled. These numbers represent unfavorable deviations from plan. The purpose of circling them is to draw immediate attention to the problem areas. This is an old and much used tactic by busy executives—focusing attention on the problem areas only; it is referred to as management by exception.

Pittsburgh's one circled number is an indication that direct labor levels exceed budget. In this case, their 110 direct labor employees is over the allotted 105 people. Houston's indirect labor level of 160 recorded for the current week and its 151 YTD both exceed the budget of 150 employees. Direct labor is also over budget, in this instance by five people. Explanations for the deviations are contained in the section of the report marked, "Comments" located at the bottom of Figure 3-2.

PMD, as a division, and despite the troubled performance being turned in by its Houston plant, is well within budgeted manpower limits. Its total employment of 630 people (Actual YTD), as seen in the bottom of the vertical column labeled, "Total Employees," is 10 people below the budgeted number of 640 people.

Now, back to budgeted vs. actual machine hours. Assume, for the moment, that the bottom dropped out of PMD's market and, as a consequence, actual machine hours YTD had been just 75% of budgeted machine hours. Here, PMD would have referred to its flexible Manpower and Standard Hour Budget to determine needed levels of manpower for that particular lowered quantity of machine hours. Remember, PMD management had prepared different budgets based on different levels of business activity. PMD would then have had a plan to cope with reduced business activity, in this case 75% lower machine hours.

The Weekly Manpower Report would then have shown lowered numbers of employees in its horizontal columns labeled "Budget YTD" and would have required actual manpower counts to be no greater than the newer, reduced numbers. In such a fashion, PMD is able to assure that manpower used almost never exceeds manpower required; and when it does, PMD management is in a good position to identify the troubled area, and to take timely and effective corrective action.

Preparation of a flexible budget, and control of manpower based on that budget, is a necessary prerequisite of dynamic profit plans. The manufacturing manager who uses the Weekly Manpower Report can assure himself that manpower levels will match profit plan expectations. Without this type of control, manpower costs are almost inevitably excessive.

The Weekly Manpower Analysis is a control tool used by the plant manager to keep manpower levels within budget. Its purpose is similar to the Weekly Manpower Report used by the manufacturing manager, except that it is aimed at the plant rather than divisional level and it contains a greater amount of detail. Figure 3-3 is such a report for the Houston plant.

The report categorizes employees by direct labor, indirect labor, and salaried employees.

INTERNATIONAL MACHINERY, INC.
PARTS MANUFACTURING DIVISION
WEEKLY MANPOWER ANALYSIS
9/30/81

PLANT: HOUSTON

BUDGETED MACHINE HOURS YTD   382,500

ACTUAL MACHINE HOURS YTD   382,800

	THIS WEEK	ACTUAL YTD	BUDGET YTD	LAST YEAR
DIRECT LABOR	200	190	195	200
INDIRECT LABOR				
Maintenance	28	28	28	37
Inspectors	(29)	(23)	22	25
Tool Grinders	14	14	14	15
Machinists	20	20	20	25
Cranemen	12	12	12	12
Material Handlers	(30)	28	28	34
Guards	5	5	5	5
Setup Men	12	12	12	12
Leadmen	(10)	9	9	10
Total	(160)	(151)	150	175
SALARIED EMPLOYEES				
Plant Manager	1	1	1	1
Secretary/clerks	1	1	1	1
Superintendents	2	2	2	2
Production Control	4	4	4	4
Mfg. Engineering	10	9	10	5
Foremen	12	12	12	12
Total	30	29	30	25
GRAND TOTAL: ALL EMPLOYEES:	(390)	370	375	400

Figure 3-3. Parts Manufacturing Division: Weekly manpower analysis.

If you will recall from Figure 3-2, Houston had five direct labor employees over budget, and ten indirect labor employees over budget. An analysis of Figure 3-3 will quickly show where the variances lie, at least for the indirect labor variance. (Variances for direct labor are ascertained through study of the plant's productivity by departments. Refer to Chapter 2).

The circled numbers tell the story. For indirect labor, Houston has 29 inspectors on board for the current week compared with 22 inspectors budgeted YTD. They have 30 material handlers compared with the budgeted number of 28, and there are 10 leadmen working while the budget permits only nine.

Houston has 200 direct labor employees compared with a budgeted figure of 195, but their actual YTD is 190—well within the budget. Should they continue to hold the 200 direct labor employees, Houston will soon find itself pressing the budgeted limit. The current number of 200 direct labor people constitutes a danger signal for the plant manager. That number will have to be reduced unless production levels increase. The plant manager is aware that machine hours are basically on target. The top of the Weekly Manpower Analysis contains the budgeted and actual machine hours for the year-to-date. Notice that both numbers are very close. This is a signal to the plant manager that he will definitely need to reduce the direct labor headcount by five people.

Looking at the totals displayed at the bottom of Figure 3-3 in the horizontal column named "Grand Total: All Employees," it is evident that Houston has 390 people on board for the current week. That is 15 above the YTD budget of 375. They have fewer than the 400 employees for the previous year, and their actual YTD of 370 is marginally below the budget. An astute plant manager, in this instance, will find a way to shed his plant of the extra 15 people so he can operate with a fair safety margin. Running as close to the budget as he is, a small drop in actual machine hours might cause Houston to soon be over manpower limits for that lower level of business.

4
Slashing Labor Costs with Short-Interval Scheduling

"There is one thing stronger than all the armies in the world; and that is an idea whose time has come."

Victor Hugo

Probably the greatest problem (and opportunity) for today's manufacturing manager is the reduction of costs; and, in labor intensive companies such as PMD, that means cutting labor costs. The last chapter showed you how to budget and control labor costs; this chapter will explain one of the most effective techniques to reduce manpower. It's called short-interval scheduling.

Short-interval scheduling (SIS) is a technique that has been used successfully by a multitude of companies to increase production with fewer employees. In its most basic form, SIS is a method of assigning employees planned quantities of work to be completed by a specific time. It then provides a means to determine that the quantities of work have been completed within the specified time limit.

In SIS, the most common interval of time assigned to complete a job is one hour, but that will vary according to the type of work and its technical complexity. More on this subject later. The entire concept of SIS, moreover, is centered about the fact that time is one of management's most precious assets. If a company can control 60 minutes in most of its hours for most of its employees, it can reduce labor costs and

Note: Parts of this chapter are based on the author's book, *Short-Interval Scheduling,* McGraw-Hill, 1968.

improve profitability. The techniques of SIS, and its repeated application by manufacturing supervisors, trains all supervisors to effectively utilize all of their available resources. It highlights operations in the manufacturing process that do not meet established standards, and ensures that manufacturing supervisors are focusing their attention on improving those operations.

TYPICAL APPLICATIONS

SIS has been used by fabricating companies, process plants, food and drug companies, steel mills, boat yards, hotels, brokerage houses, warehouses, and banks to name just a few. Successful SIS programs have been adopted in such diverse functions as production, materials handling, quality assurance, maintenance, engineering, machine shops, and assembly operations. The most frequent and productive applications have invariably been in companies where work measurement (the application of standards to work) has not yet been applied. It is there that SIS has enjoyed its greatest successes.

SIS began its existence in the fast-moving mail order business, was nurtured there, and soon expanded to a multitude of other businesses. Today, SIS is flourishing in many hundreds of American companies, and has by now been extensively implemented in companies abroad.

SIS has had great success in both direct and indirect labor applications; the technique has also been applied to the work of salaried employees engaged in routine or semiroutine jobs. Depending on the degree of control exercised over people before the installation of SIS, the technique has been known to produce labor savings of up to 60%. Savings in the range of 20% to 30% are not uncommon.

HOW SIS WORKS

SIS cannot be applied the same way from company to company; it must be tailor-made to fit the company. All SIS programs, however, would have the following elements common to them:

A. All operations to be scheduled must first be timed and the capacity of each and every work station must be determined throughout the manufacturing process.

B. The volume of work that can be comfortably handled by each work station must be determined and then production schedules can be made from that information. This step will also allow the analyst to determine manpower requirements for each station in the production process.

C. Determine how long it takes to move work through the entire manufacturing process based on the work station times derived from the steps mentioned above.

D. Only standard or regular work should be scheduled using SIS. Special jobs, work of very short duration, or highly complex work are best left handled outside of the system. This should not constitute a problem, since the vast majority of work is regular and unexceptional.

E. Staff each work station in the manufacturing process based on work standards and needed work schedules.

F. Cross-train people to handle each other's jobs. That will assure flexibility to respond to changes in the work schedule, and to provide for absentees.

G. All work entering any given manufacturing department must funnel through one dispatching station which will release work to employees of the department at predetermined intervals.

H. Control work backlogs by dispatching only that amount of work provided by the schedule. Provide for additional loads through overtime, borrowing people from another department, etc.

I. Establish the proper short-interval for dispatching work.

J. Follow all work-in-process to assure that schedules are being met.

WHY SIS WORKS

The essential ingredient of SIS is *control*. SIS controls routine and semiroutine operations because it requires periodic checks of workers' output throughout the day at brief intervals of time. It focuses management's attention continuously on production problems where schedules are not being met, and encourages manufacturing supervisors to improve their operations.

SIS instills in both supervisors and operators a sense of urgency to get the job done. The pressure to keep things on track is always there.

And it works because SIS establishes obtainable goals on a *short-range* basis. The frequent appraisals of worker performance throughout the day ensure that they will produce at or above standard levels. These short-range goals are much preferable to daily output totals measured by supervisors. When a foreman, for example, does not know what his people produced until the end of the shift, it is generally to late to take fast and effective corrective action. In manufacturing, time lost is time never regained. The best that can be hoped for normally is overtime or the hiring of additional people to provide for the mistakes made the day before.

SIS offers other advantages. These will, of course, vary from one company and one installation to another:

A. The essence of SIS is the continuous audit and examination of production operations. This surveillance inevitably results in improved operating methods, reduced costs, and higher productivity.

B. Work-in-process inventories particularly, and finished goods and raw materials inventories to some extent, are reduced to their lowest practicable minimums.

C. Manufacturing managers learn to utilize those resources at their command to the fullest; they soon begin to understand the importance of time in the manufacturing function, and learn to take maximum advantage of every working hour.

D. The SIS reporting system highlights problem areas and focuses everyone's attention on those operations that are substandard. This attention always results in improvements.

E. Most importantly, labor costs are reduced simply because with SIS it takes fewer people to do the same amount of work than was needed before the SIS installation.

THE ROLE OF SIS IN PRODUCTION PLANNING AND CONTROL

The introduction of SIS lets each manufacturing department marry its unique function to the total plan. To accomplish that, SIS must begin in the initial planning activity.

The success of installing an SIS program begins and ends in the production planning and control area. Many steps must be taken in between, but the plan must conform to the basic needs of the operation.

This is the beginning. And the plan must work on a continuous basis. This is the end result. To bring that about a very basic change must be made in the production planning and control function. The entire success of the SIS program depends on the effectiveness of that change. To understand the importance of the change, it is necessary to first outline the basic function of production planning and control, and to relate it to short-interval scheduling.

Production planning and control is the function that decrees what work shall be done, and how, when, and where it shall be done. In actual practice the planning function and the control function are separate. Planning is responsible for producing a low-cost, high-quality product. Control keeps work flowing on schedule and institutes corrective action when the plan goes off-course. If the plan is faulty or if control is ineffective, processing costs increase and delivery suffers. The company loses business and profits drop.

Because so many variables can affect the flow of work through a plant, the planning and control people are usually under pressure, and constantly feel the need to build in cushions to protect delivery dates and to prevent inventory shortages from occurring in the manufacturing operations. And quite often those cushions are accepted as needed and are used as a matter of practice. In most companies, one of two situations generally exists. In the first situation, planning loads are deliberately made light because the planning group realizes that many things can go wrong. Consequently, plant utilization is low compared with available capacity. Delays and lost time become accepted as normal.

In the second case, the planning loads are set to the absolute maximum even though the production organization constantly demonstrates its inability to come through. Replanning and frequent changes in the schedule result. This situation is just as dangerous as the first one. In both cases, accomplishments are far below the potential of the facilities and the people.

The successful SIS program is based upon realistic production planning and control. SIS controls the production departments through the production plan. If a major error is made in the production plan, it will be transmitted through the SIS system and could possibly reverse the very purpose of the SIS program. SIS, by necessity, must begin with the design of the production plan. Once that document has been perfected, the short-interval schedule can be made and installed.

SEPARATE THE RESPONSIBILITY

It is necessary to first understand an important distinction. As previously mentioned, production planning loads the manufacuring departments, and production control follows up on the progress of the schedule. Both functions are defined as the responsibility of production planning and control. SIS changes that relationship. Although the responsibility for schedule accomplishment (control) is still separated from the responsibility for schedule preparation (planning), *the sole responsibility for meeting the manufacturing schedule belongs to the foremen and their managers.*

To support that relationship, a secondary and supporting principle is made. *The first line foreman must be given a definite schedule for which he is held accountable, and that schedule should be for a short period of time.* Ideally, the schedule should indicate the total man-hours output required by labor classification and machine center so the foreman can properly allocate the workload.

Schedules are then released in short increments—for a day, three days or a week—depending on the complexity of the operation. The foreman receives only that workload scheduled for the short term. Future work stays in production planning and is released to the foreman only when he finishes the current work schedule. Receiving only the work that is required on a definite schedule eliminates the need for the foreman to operate from a priority list.

Work assignment with SIS clearly stipulates that only the foreman shall assign work to any given operator. This principle must be extended to the planning department. It assigns the workload to the foreman who, in turn, assigns work to the operator. To carry out this responsibility, it is necessary to assign the job for meeting schedule dates to the foreman. Production planning will then support the procedure by issuing sequenced production schedules on a periodic basis.

DEVELOPING AND INSTALLING SIS

The very first task to be accomplished when developing an SIS program is the installation of work standards. To establish work standards for the SIS program it is necessary to define the units of measure which are to be scheduled, and then find out how long each unit of measure takes to perform. This is termed the "job-time relationship." As the study is developed and standards are evolved, it will be noticed that SIS work standards are aimed at alerting the supervisor to recognize off-schedule conditions in the briefest practical time. These questions will be answered:

1. What does the employee do?
2. How much does he do?
3. How often does he do it?
4. How long does it take?

Rarely in any manufacturing operation that has not had work measurement applied is a foreman fully aware of what is involved and how long it takes to do a job. In a typical manufacturing operation, for example, a machine is set-up, tried-out, the first piece is inspected, material stocked, production run, material taken away, and adjustments made to the machine. Would the foreman of that operation in *your* shop be able to comprehensively describe time values for each of those activities? Or, would he be able to tell you just how many pieces were processed through that particular machine during the shift? Could he predict with some accuracy how often each product is run through the machine? Chances are he could not really do justice to those questions. *If a manufacturing foreman is to be effective on his job, however, he must know that information and know how to use it to control labor costs and productivity.* Now ask yourself why your foreman is not aware of the answers to those questions. It isn't simply because he has not been trained to cope with production problems in terms of meeting a schedule.

SIS is a new way of looking at the job-time relationship. It assures that all elements of a major nature regarding the operation are known by the foreman, and places a unique tool in his hands to control the flow of work. The unique tool, of course, is SIS. The knowledge is provided by the work standards.

THE UNIT OF MEASURE

Defining the proper unit of work to which the time standard is applied is a basic task that anybody well grounded in the fundamentals of industrial engineering should be able to do readily. Defining the unit of measure, however, is a job that is not as easy as it may first appear to be. SIS experts undertake considerable analysis and study to arrive at the proper unit of measure. Some applications are relatively easy. Others are more complex. Care must be exercised to assure that the unit of measure is a uniform measure.

In most manufacturing operations, a great deal of attention has been focused on work standards. Consequently, the activities that have been measured by work standard procedures (time study, MTM, standard data, etc.) have normally a well established unit of measure. Most of them—unfortunately—are of little value because they are expressed in terms that are hard to understand.

For example, many work standards are expressed in standard hours, which must then be transposed through mathematical calculations, to pieces per hour. The latter number is the information the foreman needs to control his operation. A production foreman has neither the time nor the inclination to convert a clumsily stated standard into something he can work with. For the foreman to use work standards to advantage, they must be converted into pieces per hour.

To help understand the basis of preparation for units of measure, the table illustrated below is a simplified version of a typical work standard sheet used by PMD's Drill Press Department:

SECTION: DRILL PRESSES

ACTIVITY	UNIT OF MEASURE	PIECES PER HOUR
Stock press	Cart	5.00 minutes
Change fixtures	Each fixture	5.00 minutes
Set-up single drill	Set-up	17.50 minutes
Set-up double drill	Set-up	29.75 minutes
Drill operations		
Single hole	piece	400
Double hole	piece	350
Single hole—both sides	piece	180
Double hole—both sides	piece	125

There is no attempt to be precise or scientifically accurate when establishing units of measure. Too much detail is really a hinderance.

An undue focus on obtaining exact units of measure inevitably results in loss of perspective. The entire purpose of SIS is to reduce payroll dollars and make the manufacturing system more dependable. Nitpicking about precise units of measure substitutes technical virtuosity for bottom line results. With SIS, whatever is lost by using larger units of measure is more than regained by the inherent payroll savings.

In the table illustrated above, the first four jobs are expressed in minutes for completion rather than pieces per hour. Because these jobs occur but infrequently, the jobs themselves become the units of measure, and the time required to perform the jobs become the work standards. It would be impractical, if not downright silly, for example, to express "stock press" as occurring twelve times per hour when, in actuality, the stocking of work at each drill press occurs but three times per shift.

The bottom four activities shown in the table are capable of being expressed as "pieces" the most appropriate and simplest unit of measure. The work standards are then easily expressed as so many pieces per hour—work standards foremen and operators alike can understand and use.

There are a few basic principles that can be used for selection of units of measure. These are:

1. The unit selected should be the broadest and most uniform possible.
2. It must be that type of unit that can be expressed in pieces per hour (unless, of course, it is nonrepetitive).
3. If any type of paperwork is involved, the unit of measure should be located in the source document itself.
4. It must be easily measured to save the foreman's time when checking work.

THE REASONABLE EXPECTANCY

Work standards in SIS are termed "reasonable expectancies." A reasonable expectancy is that quantity of work that can be produced by an average employee under normal working conditions in a given period of time. The period of time is generally one hour, but can vary depending on the application.

The reasonable expectancy is defined in terms of the unit of measure. In a data processing operation, for example, the punch card becomes the unit of measure in the key punch section. The reasonable expectancy would be expressed as the number of cards that can be run by one key punch operator in one hour.

Whenever reasonable expectancies are being determined, the following ground rules apply:

1. The job being studied must be tested under normal working conditions. No attempt should be made to isolate the operator or impose ideal working conditions if the expected measurement is to be representative.
2. The operator being studied should be working at a reasonable pace.
3. As with all work standards, enough studies should be taken to assure accuracy of the data. In highly repetitive operations five to ten observations will be adequate, depending on the complexity of the work elements. In less repetitive jobs additional observations will be necessary.
4. Historical data should seldom be used as a basis for determining reasonable expectancies. Those data might contain lost time or other elements foreign to the operation at hand.
5. "Pure time" will constitute the reasonable expectancy. Pure time is the time needed to perform a given job, exclusive of all unusual forms of lost time.

The reasonable expectancy is quite different from the usual exact standards commonly used in most manufacturing operations. The standards presently in use contain built-in allowances for various delays; whereas reasonable expectancies do not. When a "batch" of reasonable expectancies are assigned to an operator, he is being told to perform a reasonable amount of work for the given time period. No attempt is made to speed-up his activity. Neither is he allowed the luxury of built-in wasted time. He is expected to do a fair day's work. The reasonable expectancy stresses output rather than the work measurement tool itself. SIS emphasizes scheduling and control as the key factors in obtaining increased output and operational efficiencies.

THE ACTIVITY REPORT

In almost any manufacturing operation, the major portion of the work-load consists primarily of a few major tasks. For example, the major task of a drill press operaor is drilling. The remaining time is devoted to subsidiary tasks such as set-up, inspection, machine adjustments, and writing production tallies. It is the job of the Activity Report to specify those tasks and to record how often and when they are performed. The Activity Report is the basis for determining the total workload of the production operator, and serves as the basis for the determination of reasonable expectancies.

Figure 4-1 is PMD's Activity Report used to determine the workload of one of its automatic chucker operators. To start the report, all job duties are listed on the left side of the sheet. It is best to have them described in simple terms. Next, the units of measure are listed opposite their activities.

The right side of the sheet is divided into time periods. About four

PLANT : PITTSBURGH DEPARTMENTS : CHUCKERS	PARTS MANUFACTURING DIVISION ACTIVITY REPORT					DATE : 6/25 SHIFT : #1 FOREMAN : J. GIVENS OPERATOR : P. MARTIN	
	UNIT OF MEASURE	VOLUME					
DESCRIPTION OF ACTIVITY		7 AM –9 AM	9 AM –11 AM	11.30 AM –1.30PM	1.30 PM –3.30 PM		TOTALS
Operate chucker	Piece	210	55	130	162		557
Set-up chucker	Set-up		1				1
Adjust chucker	Adjustment	2	7	3	1		13
Clean-out scrap	Scrap tub		1		1		2
Write production tally	Card	2	1	2	2		7
Layout parts	Part						0
Inspect parts	Piece	15	3	15	15		48

Figure 4-1. Parts Manufacturing Division: Activity report.

periods have been found to be adequate for purposes of this type of study. When the described work has been performed, the operator places a hash mark in the proper column opposite the task performed. The exception to this is actual production itself. In that case, the operator simply records production output for the time period. Numbers instead of hash marks have been used in Figure 4-1 to clarify the example. But in actual practice, hash marks are preferable for all activities other than actual production; they do not leave anything to the operator's memory.

At the conclusion of the shift, the Activity Report is collected by the foreman and a fresh report is issued the following day. This tally should be completed by each production operator for about three or four weeks. Again, if the job is highly repetitive, three weeks or less will suffice. If there are many nonroutine tasks to be done, four weeks is better. By then sufficient data will have been gathered to indicate all of the operator's responsibilities and their frequencies of occurrence.

During the period of time when the Activity Report is being maintained, the SIS observer should be determining work standards for all of the jobs listed on the report. The guidelines for establishing reasonable expectancies should be used. Time studies can be used to establish work standards, although many SIS practitioners use a wrist watch or wall clock. The differences are not important. Exactness is not required. What is important is that the time established be considered "pure time." It should not include time when the employee is waiting for work, or time when unusual interruptions occur.

Once reasonable expectancies are set, the work should be "batched" and assigned to employees. Batching is the physical accumulation of work into usually one hour portions. After assignment, the employee doing the work should be checked several times to verify the accuracy of the reasonable expectancies.

Work standards are now ready to be applied to the operations. The Activity Report is used to arrive at the amount of time required to handle the volume of work. These data provide the necessary information to manload each production station and schedule each employee. They are also used to establish the correct crew size for every scheduled operation in the department.

Using the Activity Report as the source of information, a new Activity Report—as seen in Figure 4-2—is prepared. All activities are listed on the left side of the report, as before. Units of measure follow, also as before. Reasonable expectancies are added to this report, as seen in the third column. Instead of time periods of the report shown in Figure 4-2, the volume of work performed is summarized and displayed in the fourth column.

Reasonable expectancies are then multiplied by the volume of work accomplished—in the "Volume" column, each occurence represents a hash mark from the previous Activity Report—and the resultant total time is pure, uninterrupted work time in which to perform that quantity of work for each day.

All activity volumes are totaled for that day and the resultant time represents the actual workload. This will provide reliable information concerning the amount of work accomplished each day vs. the available time to accomplish the work. Those numbers are shown on the bottom of the new Activity Report. "Total Time Working" is arrived at by

PLANT : PITTSBURGH DEPARTMENT : CHUCKERS	PARTS MANUFACTURING DIVISION ACTIVITY REPORT		DATE : 6/25 SHIFT : #1 FOREMAN : J . GIVENS OPERATOR : P . MARTIN	
DESCRIPTION OF ACTIVITY	UNIT OF MEASURE	REASONABLE EXPECTANCY	VOLUME	TOTAL TIME
Operate chucker	Piece	0.2 Minutes	557	111.4 Minutes
Set-up chucker	Set-up	60.0 Minutes	1	60.0 Minutes
Adjust chucker	Adjustment	2.0 Minutes	13	26.0 Minutes
Clean-out scrap	Scrap tub	3.0 Minutes	2	6.0 Minutes
Write production tally	Card	1.0 Minutes	7	7.0 Minutes
Layout parts	Part	30.0 Minutes	0	0 Minutes
Inspect parts	Piece	0.2 Minutes	48	9.6 Minutes
Totals:			⟶	220.0 Minutes

$$\text{Total Time Working} = \frac{\text{Total Time Working}}{450 \text{ Minutes}} = \frac{220 \text{ Minutes}}{450 \text{ Minutes}} \times 100 = 48.9\%$$

$$\text{Total Time Operating} = \frac{\text{Total Time Operating}}{450 \text{ Minutes}} = \frac{111.4 \text{ Minutes}}{450 \text{ Minutes}} \times 100 = 24.8\%$$

Figure 4-2. Parts Manufacturing Division: Activity report summary.

dividing the total time worked, found in the right-hand column, by 450 minutes. The number 450 (minutes) is derived by subtracting from 480 minutes (8 hours × 60 minutes per hour) allowances for breaks and get-ready and clean-up time, generally 30 minutes. Notice that the operator of the automatic chucker being studied for that day worked only 48.9% of the time. That result is not unusual in any production operation where work measurement has not been applied, and where foremen have not been trained to think in terms of management of time in their jobs.

The key figure, "Total Time Operating," shown immediately below "Total Time Working" is an indication of just how much time the chucker is actually cranking out production parts. This number is found by dividing the time the chucker was operating—see activity marked "Operate Chucker"—by 450 minutes. In this case, the chucker was actually turning-out parts only 24.8% of the shift. Again, this number is not unusual in many manufacturing operations where work measurement and schedules have not been properly used.

All activity volumes for the entire department under study are summarized. Usually, at this stage, it becomes apparent that a surprising excess of time is either being lost or wasted. For an eight-hour shift, it is not unusual for work accomplishment to be under 50% while actual operating time is no higher than 30%.

Summation of Activity Reports will provide the basis for future reduction of manpower. When the SIS program is installed, those reductions can be realized.

THE SIGN-OUT

Once reasonable expectancies and workloads have been established, it is necessary to break down projected workloads into daily increments. Some procedure must be devised to assign the work to individual machine operators and work stations. This is the principle of dispatching work. It is called "sign-out."

Sign-out indicates the assignment of work to operators in quantities that have been converted to a total time requirement for each assignment. In manufacturing, "batching" of work is quite common. The

Batch Ticket displayed in Figure 4-3 is a typical document used to dispatch and assign work in manufacturing operations.

Following the principle of sign-out in its entirety, each batch of work would have a Batch Ticket when distributed to employees. SIS has been successful because an operator knows before he starts when a batch of work should be completed. The Batch Ticket does that. It communicates the production goal and work standard to the operator and lets him know when he is required to complete the work in hand. It also lets the operator talk to his foreman about any obstacles he might anticipate which could prevent him from completing the work in the stipulated time.

The batch ticket shown in Figure 4-3 tells the operator how long it takes to run one piece (cycle time), how long the production run should take, and how much time is alloted for a set-up to complete the lot of work. Any delays he might encounter are to be enumerated on the batch ticket also.

Most traditional forms of work measurement lack the direct com-

DATE: 6/25 SHIFT: #2

AUTOMATIC CHUCKER DEPARTMENT BATCH TICKET

LOT NUMBER	PART	ORDER QUANTITY	CYCLE TIME	PIECES PER HOUR	SET - UP TIME	RUN TIME	TOTAL LOT TIME
2157	2″ Plug	360	60 Sec	60	1.5 Hrs	6 Hrs	7.5 Hrs

Operator	Set-up Time		Run Time		
	Start	Stop	Start	Stop	Number Good Pieces Run
P. Martin	7:00 AM	8:05 AM	8:05 AM	3:30 PM	365

Delays	From	To	Comments
Operator's adjustments Machinist's adjustments Electrician's adjustments Lubricate chucker Wait for stocker Wait for crane Quality problems Other(write in)	1:20 PM	1:30 PM	Burr on part—tool changed

Figure 4-3. Parts Manufacturing Division: Batch ticket.

munication between operator and foreman at the job level or work station producing the goods. Also, most operators do not know how well they have done according to established work standards. Even at daily intervals, when an operator is apprised of his performance, it is usually done in a very general way with little or no discussion of how well he performed on specific assignments. The real loss is that the foreman does not know in time to take remedial action, neither is he aware of how much additional work an operator is ready to assume. SIS solves those problems and improves production rates above that which may not be realized under the traditional forms of work measurement.

THE SCHEDULE CONTROL

For the foreman to control the work after the operator has been informed of the goal, another tool must be made available to him. This tool is the core of the short-interval scheduling program. It is called the "Schedule Control." This document keeps the foreman informed of the progress of the schedule on a timely basis. The foreman can plan ahead to remain on schedule, even when falling behind because of additional workloads.

Figure 4-4 is a modified schedule control adopted by PMD's Automatic Chucker Department. The left-hand side of the form lists the operators' names. The time periods across the top are divided into four, two-hour intervals of the normal working shift, plus two, one-hour intervals for planning overtime. There is room to enter both planned and actual production on the form. Two-hour rather than one-hour intervals were selected as the most appropriate in this particular example.

Using the batch tickets, the foreman observes the number of pieces per hour required, doubles that figure (for the two-hour cycle) and records that amount in the space marked "P" opposite each operator listed on the form. He then extends the planned quantities into as many time periods as needed, depending on the quantity to be scheduled. A sufficient quantity of Batch Tickets should be calculated for each operation to fill the working shift.

Every two hours the foreman checks the work output of each operator at his work station. He enters actual production in the space marked "A" for that operation. The foreman then adds the planned quantities

EMPLOYEE	PLAN ACTUAL	7:00 AM TO 9:00 AM	9:00 AM TO 11:00 AM	11:30 AM TO 1:30 PM	1:30 PM TO 3:30 PM	3:30 PM TO 4:30 PM	4:30 PM TO 5:30 PM
		AUTOMATIC CHUCKER DEPARTMENT SCHEDULE CONTROL					
Burke	P	150	150	150	150		
	A	(128)	150	150	160		
Morton	P	100	100	300	300		
	A	100	100	(250)	360		
Green	P	200	200	150	200		
	A	200	200	180	200		
Jackson	P	50	50	50	50		
	A	60	58	54	59		
Morrison	P	70	70	80	80		
	A	70	70	80	80		
Bi-Hourly Total	P	570	570	730	780		
	A	(558)	578	(714)	859		
Cumulative Total	P	570	1140	1870	2690		
	A	(558)	(1136)	(1850)	2709		

Figure 4-4. Parts Manufacturing Division: Schedule control.

for that time period and enters them in the "P" section of the column titled "Bi-Hourly Total." He does the same for the actual production figures. The column marked "Cumulative Total" represents the cumulative totals of the columns marked "Bi-Hourly Total." The foreman can now measure each operation and the performance of the entire department. He can recognize off-schedule conditions and take corrective action. If behind, he can plan overtime or borrow extra operators. If ahead of schedule he can plan additional work to stay ahead of the schedule. What is important is that he can do all this before the end of the day. SIS prevents losing time that can never be regained.

Figure 4-4 clearly illustrates that point. In the Schedule Control PMD supervisors have circled all actual production quantities that were below planned quantities. Notice that for the first two-hour period the bi-hourly totals fell behind schedule. The second period improved but not enough to bring the cumulative total up to plan for the first four hours of the shift. The third bi-hourly total also fell below schedule which further deteriorated the cumulative total. In the last two-hour period of the day, however, the foreman's section produced more than enough production to offset earlier losses and end the shift above plan. Had the foreman been unaware that he was falling behind schedule hour-by-hour he most probably would not have taken aggressive corrective action to improve production and meet the schedule.

FINDING THE BEST SHORT-INTERVAL

The importance of finding the best short-interval of time to control a production operation cannot be minimized. There are no hard-and-fast rules governing the selection of the optimum interval. The length of time will vary from situation to situation.

Good judgment must be used. In a high production and repetitive operation the short-interval might be one hour. In a complex assembly operation which has few repetitive features, two- to four-hour intervals would be more suitable. In the fast-moving mail order business, where SIS has its roots, twenty-minute intervals are not uncommon.

The interval, to be effective, must not consume excess supervisory time. Yet it must be taken often enough to control operations. The guidelines many SIS practitioners use to establish practical short-intervals of control are:

1. The duration must be short enough to permit corrective action to be taken in time to keep the schedule current.
2. It must not take an excessive amount of time for the foreman to devote to that task.
3. The interval must be short enough to motivate the operator to achieve the goal.

UNSCHEDULED WORK

A certain amount of work cannot be scheduled feasibly and assigned reasonable expectancies. This amount will vary according to the task to be done. Each task must be judged by its individual merits. The reason that some nonroutine or unusual work cannot be scheduled is because work standards cannot be established and used practically. If the work is occasional or small; if there are a very large number of small batches; if the work is highly nonroutine—then the work does not lend itself to practical scheduling. Too much time would need to be devoted to control a very minor proportion of the workload.

While work standards can be applied to just about anything, there are some instances where the cost of applying them is prohibitive. Nonroutine work of this nature can best be handled outside of the SIS system. As a rule, if SIS can cover about 80% of the operations, that is all that is needed to produce substantial labor savings.

5
Staffing and Controlling Indirect Labor Functions

"For purposes of action nothing is more useful than narrowness of thought combined with energy of will."

Henri Frédéric Amiel

The previous two chapters described effective methods that have been used successfully to control and reduce manpower costs. While those methods are appropriate for both direct labor and indirect labor alike, the staffing and control of indirect labor functions sometimes demands different approaches and the application of special techniques. This chapter describes those approaches and techniques. These are:

1. The use of standard direct labor hours to staff and control indirect labor functions.
2. The application of work sampling to measure indirect labor functions.
3. The design of "plateau" charts to staff indirect labor functions.

THE STANDARD HOUR METHOD OF CONTROL

Many manufacturing companies have found that the comparison of indirect labor hours to direct labor standard hours is their best way to staff and control indirect labor functions. Using historical direct labor hours and indirect labor hours, budgets for the approaching fiscal year are determined for different levels of business. Figure 5-1, PMD's "Indirect Labor Control" sheet is a typical example of how standard hours are used to budget indirect labor functions.

The report in Figure 5-1 is issued weekly and, in this case, reflects indirect labor hours for PMD's Houston plant. The vertical column heads are explained here:

Direct Labor Standard Hours are the number of direct labor hours earned based on the number of parts produced. A study of Chapter 3 will show specifically how these hours are derived.

Standard Indirect Labor Hours are the number of indirect hours · budgeted at the level of direct labor standard hours shown in the first column.

Actual Indirect Labor Hours are the actual number of indirect labor hours generated during the week.

Variances are the differences between actual and standard indirect labor hours for the week being examined.

INTERNATIONAL MACHINERY, INC.
PARTS MANUFACTURING DIVISION
INDIRECT LABOR CONTROL

Plant: Houston   **Date: 9/30/81**

WEEK ENDING	DIRECT LABOR STANDARD HOURS	INDIRECT LABOR HOURS STANDARD	ACTUAL	VARIANCES	EQUIVALENT PEOPLE
9/2	7790	5843	6208	(365)	9.1
9/9	7850	5888	6220	(332)	8.3
9/16	7990	5993	6212	(219)	5.5
9/23	8010	6008	6490	(482)	12.1
9/30	8020	6075	6480	(405)	10.1

Notes: Indirect labor hours as a percentage of direct labor hours have been established as follows:

Direct Labor Hours	Indirect Labor Percentage
4000–4999	79%
5000–5999	77
6000–6999	76
7000–7999	75
8000–8999	75
9000–9999	73

Comments: Refer to Weekly Manpower Analysis for definitive manpower reduction plans to bring indirect labor hours in line with direct labor hours (Chapter 3).

Figure 5-1. Parts Manufacturing Divsion: Indirect labor control.

Equivalent People is derived by dividing the hours found in the "Variances" column by 40 hours—the number of hours worked by one indirect labor employee in one week.

The week of 9/2, for example, shows that 7790 direct labor hours were earned. 5843 indirect labor hours were budgeted for that period. The *actual* number of indirect labor hours produced was 6208. So, the variance (in this case unfavorable) is:

6208 Actual Hours — 5843 Standard Hours = 365 Hours

Equivalent people is then found by dividing 365 hours by 40 hours:

$$\frac{365 \text{ Hours}}{40 \text{ Hours}} = 9.1 \text{ Equivalent People}$$

PMD Houston, then, had 9.1 indirect labor people over budget for the week ending September 1.

To determine standard indirect labor hours, Houston has examined its historical records and correlated indirect labor hours to differing levels of direct labor hours. The result is found under "Notes" in Figure 5-1. At the direct labor level of 7000–7999 hours, for example, it has been found that indirect labor hours will be about 75% of direct labor hours.

Notice that as direct labor hours increase, the percentage of indirect labor hours decrease. This is as it should be. When production volume increases, it should take fewer indirect labor hours proportionately to support that increase.

A case in point is Houston's Milling Machine Department. One inspector (a typical indirect labor activity) serviced 15 milling machines. When production volume increased, one inspector was able to cover 20 milling machines, with but minor modifications to his work methods.

In most production activities, moderate increases in volume almost always are absorbed by existing indirect labor employees. When the increases are more substantial, indirect people are then added, but seldom at the level of the number of direct labor people added. To add one indirect labor employee for every direct labor employee added would be sheer folly. It would soon bankrupt the company.

The "Comments" section shown at the bottom of Figure 5-1 reflects corrective action being taken to reduce the level of indirect labor employees. *All* reports displaying negative trends should contain specific corrective actions.

USING WORK SAMPLING TO MEASURE INDIRECT LABOR

Once that indirect labor hours have been estimated for varying levels of business through use of historical records, some method should be devised to establish the accuracy of the numbers. In most manufacturing activities, use of historical records to establish standards normally results in wasted manpower. The historical information simply brings forward the mistakes made in the past. If little or no control was exercised over indirect labor in the past, a projection of hours needed based on past data will reproduce the same mistakes in the present and in the future. The budget will reflect an excess of indirect labor employees needed to do the job.

But historical data represent a good place to begin the planning cycle. They have the advantage of getting you off to a good start. Now let's observe one of the best ways to determine indirect labor workloads. It's called work sampling, and to a large extent, it's even a better method for measuring indirect labor activity than short-interval scheduling. (Remember, SIS is better applied to highly repetitive and routine work. Indirect labor functions are classified as semirepetitive work.)

Work sampling is a random sampling method where periodic observations of employees are used to measure the extent of their activities. It can be contrasted to time study, and other basic methods of work measurement, where continuous observations are necessary. In work sampling, only limited numbers of observations are needed daily to reveal workload patterns.

Using work sampling, PMD, Houston, monitored its 25 inspectors during September and October of 1981 to see if the budgeted indirect labor hours for quality assurance was realistic. Industrial engineers walked through the factory daily at predetermined random times to observe what activities inspectors were performing. The activities observed were recorded on the form shown in Figure 5-2.

The "Random Times" column contains predetermined sampling times as taken directly from a table of random numbers. (Available in

INTERNATIONAL MACHINERY, INC.
PARTS MANUFACTURING DIVISION
WORK SAMPLING FORM

Plant: Houston

Date: 9/6

RANDOM TIMES	FIRST PIECE INSPECTION	LOT INSPECTION	GAGE CALIBRATION	TRAVEL TIME	TALK TO: FOREMAN	TALK TO: OPER.	PREP. TIME	PERSONAL
7:05AM							X	
7:40AM								X
8:18AM				X				
8:50AM								X
9:00AM								X
9:30AM					X			
10:03AM		X						
10:19AM		X						
11:12AM					X			
11:28AM								X
12:20PM			X					
12:57PM	X							
1:12PM	X							
1:19PM						X		
2:16PM								X
2:48PM		X						
3:03PM		X						
3:25PM								X
Total Observations, 18	2	4	1	1	2	1	1	6

Figure 5-2. Parts Manufacturing Division: Work sampling form.

just about any book on statistics; you can even make up your own. The important point to remember is that the observation times need to be unbiased.)

The industrial engineers would then record what individual inspectors were doing at the time they were being observed. The work sampling format should always contain headings which include all of the work and nonwork elements the employees do. In this case, the headings contain inclusive work elements ranging from "First Piece Inspection" to "Personal."

At the conclusion of the day, each work sampling form is summarized and filed away for eventual compilation of the study.

The number of observations needed must be carefully determined before the study begins because it has a bearing on the accuracy of the results. The larger the number of observations, the greater the degree of accuracy. Obviously, when thousands of observations are needed to obtain a finite degree of accuracy, the manager of the work sampling study must consider practicalities—how much will the study cost vs. the degree of accuracy required? No manufacturing manager can afford to be a purist and demand statistical purity. The costs may be too prohibitive.

Glance at Figure 5-3 for a good example of some sample sizes required by theoretical work sampling. There are numbers ranging up to 158,400. Pretty large, isn't it? Not too many manufacturing organizations can afford the time and money to achieve statistical immaculacy.

We will return to Figure 5-3 for a full explanation of its contents shortly.

In a short-cycle repetitive operation not too many observations are

INTERNATIONAL MACHINERY, INC.
PARTS MANUFACTURING DIVISION
WORK SAMPLING TABLE

ESTIMATE OF OCCURRENCES	REQUIRED NUMBER OF OBSERVATIONS	
	5% ERROR FACTOR	10% ERROR FACTOR
1 %	158,400	39,600
5 %	30,400	7,600
10 %	14,400	3,600
20 %	6,400	1,600
30 %	3,680	920
40 %	2,400	600
50 %	1,600	400

Figure 5-3. Parts Manufacturing Division: Work sampling table showing required number of observations.

required. The opposite is required in the nonrepetitive activity where elements needed to be observed in the study do not occur frequently.

To determine the number of observations needed in the study, it is first necessary to estimate the percentage of occurrence of the main element you are measuring. In PMD Houston's case, industrial engineers were studying inspectors, and the main element involved was inspection time (both lot and first piece inspection). The industrial engineers conducting the study estimated that the combined inspection time would range from 40 to 50% of the time. Going to Figure 5-3 they looked at the columns titled, "5% Error Factor," and "10% Error Factor." Using the number of observations in their respective columns, it means there will be only 5 chances in 100 or 10 chances in 100 of getting a false indication of activity from the specified number of observations.

Quite obviously, should you elect to obtain a result not more than 5% wrong, the sample size will be considerably higher than a study requiring no more than a 10% error.

Since Houston desired an error factor no greater than 5% for their work sampling study of inspectors, and since the estimate of occurrences between 40 to 50% fell between the 1600 and 2400 sample size in the "5% Error Factor" column, Houston decided on taking about 2000 samples—the halfway point between 1600 and 2400.

The study was conducted over 40 working days. For a total of 2000 observations the study would need about 50 observations per day. Three industrial engineers were selected to perform the study, each taking about 16–20 observations per day.

Summarizing Work Sampling

This is the final step conducted in the study, and the most revealing one. As shown in Figure 5-4 the study indicated that Houston's inspectors had a great deal of time to spare. The results by category are displayed at the top of Figure 5-4. The summary, shown below on the report, indicates that about one-third of the inspectors' time is *totally* wasted and that other efficiencies could be obtained through some solid methods work.

Since Houston carried about 24 inspectors at the time the study was made, the conclusion was inevitable—*there were 8 more inspectors than*

INTERNATIONAL MACHINERY, INC.
PARTS MANUFACTURING DIVISION
WORK SAMPLING SUMMARY

Plant: Houston   Department: Quality Assurance
Dates of Study: 9/1–11/1

CATEGORY	NUMBER OF OBSERVATIONS	PERCENT OF TOTAL
First piece inspection	120	5.8
Lot inspection	485	23.6
Gage calibration	135	6.6
Travel time	279	13.6
Talk to foremen	132	6.4
Talk to operator	151	7.3
Preparation time	62	3.0
Personal	694	33.7
Totals:	2058	100.0%

Summary:
1. Only 29.4% of the inspectors' time was actually spent inspecting product during the study:
First piece inspection	5.8%
Lot inspection	23.6%
Total:	29.4%
2. 33.7% of inspectors; time was totally wasted.
3. Travel time was 13.6%. An improved method showing a new work path for inspectors would gain considerable time for more essential duties.

Figure 5-4. Parts Manufacturing Division: Work sampling summary.

needed. The extra people were, in effect, a penalty Houston was paying for *ineffective control* of the inspection work force. Shortly after the conclusion of the study, the 8 inspectors were removed from the inspection work force, and new methods were instituted to improve inspection efficiency.

"Plateau" Charts for Staffing

Once the work sampling study has been concluded and the numbers tabulated, it soon becomes apparent that indirect labor workloads can be more accurately planned through use of "plateau" charts. Houston's

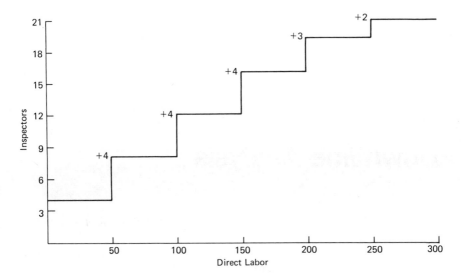

Figure 5-5. Parts Manufacturing Division: Plateau chart.

plateau chart for staffing inspectors vs. direct labor employees is displayed in Figure 5-5.

The horizontal axis represents numbers of direct labor people while the vertical axis represents numbers of inspectors. Notice the irregular "plateau" curve connecting the two. Here it can be readily seen that when certain additions to the direct labor work force are made, the number of inspectors remains constant. No additions are made to the inspection work force until the next plateau is reached.

The plateau curve is derived by workload knowledge discovered during the work sampling study combined with historical data and a liberal sprinkling of plain commonsense. The work sampling study is the basic guide. From its conclusions, inspection workloads can be devised for all levels of business. If historical data, for example, reveal that 15 inspectors were being used to service 120 direct labor employees sometime in the past, then the industrial engineer might possibly conclude that that number should be reduced to 10 inspectors servicing 120 operators. That reduction is approximately one-third, and if you will recall the work sampling study, inspectors were not working approximately one-third of the time. Therefore, it might be possible to reduce inspection ranks by the same percentage at other levels of business.

6
Downtime Analysis

"I wish I could stand on a busy corner, hat in hand, and beg people to throw me all their wasted hours."

Bernard Berenson

One of the very useful by-products of both direct and indirect labor control is the realization that downtime must be quantified and categorized so that it can be reduced. If nothing else, the preceding chapters should have made it quite clear that the more useful information the manufacturing manager has at his disposal, the more productive his efforts to control and reduce costs are likely to be.

Once that direct labor hours are categorized by "time on production" and "time on nonproduction," it soon becomes abundantly clear that "time on nonproduction" tasks absorb approximately one-quarter to half of all direct labor hours available. Given the nature of most manufacturing operations, that is really not surprising. The enormous number of variables affecting men, machines, and materials converge and create any number of possibilities of problems. And if labor has had no direct control exercised over its function, the amount of downtime is going to be even greater. In uncontrolled labor situations, management is just not aware of the extent of its downtime problems. They must be identified and quantified before any real impact is felt on the problems.

DIVISIONAL DOWNTIME SUMMARIES

There are many potential methods of gathering downtime information for analysis. The batch ticket described in Chapter 4 is a example; others include reporting delays to timekeepers, or the relatively newer shop floor control systems where operators punch data cards in terminals located in the manufacturing departments. The information gathered at the terminals includes the time each production machine is down and the reason. Computers then compile and report downtime information from each shop floor terminal.

Whatever the source, downtime information needs to be disseminated at both plant and divisional level. Information needed by the manufacturing manager is pictured in Figure 6-1, PMD's divisional level downtime analysis report.

The report is presented in two sections: (a) Summary, and (b) Detail Analysis. The summary describes, by total division and individual plant, the number of direct labor hours used on production, and the number of direct labor hours wasted on downtime. For the week ending August 20, Houston had the lowest downtime at 14.0% of direct labor hours, and Los Angeles the worst at 38.0%.

Obviously, something went wrong at Los Angeles, but what? The next section—"Detail Analysis"—explains what happened.

INTERNATIONAL MACHINERY, INC.
PARTS MANUFACTURING DIVISION
DOWNTIME ANALYSIS

Week Ending: 8/20

A. SUMMARY	HOUSTON	PITTSBURGH	LOS ANGELES	TOTAL PLANTS
Total direct labor hours worked	8,163	4,015	2,725	14,903
Direct labor hours on production	7,018	2,996	1,690	11,704
Direct labor hours on downtime	1,145	1,019	1,035	3,199
Percent downtime	14.0%	25.4%	38.0%	21.5%
B. DETAIL ANALYSIS (in Direct Labor Man-Hours).				
Set-up	215	139	181	535
Machine adjustments	190	112	131	433
Rework	306	265	175	746
Wait time—materials	28	94	60	182
Machine repairs	253	285	312	850
Tooling repairs	153	116	136	405
Training	0	8	40	48
Totals:	1,145	1,019	1,035	3,199

Figure 6-1. Parts Manufacturing Division: Downtime analysis.

Under "Detail Analysis," general categories of downtime are listed. Notice the relatively large amount of direct labor hours Los Angeles lost on machine repairs. In fact, the amount of time Los Angeles lost for set-up, machine adjustments, and tooling repairs are very high in comparison to its sister plants when you consider that Los Angeles' total number of direct labor hours worked are smaller.

Tooling repairs for the three plants, for example, when considered as a percentage of their direct labor hours worked, looks like this:

$$\text{Houston } \frac{153 \text{ Hours}}{8163 \text{ Hours}} \times 100 = 1.9\%$$

$$\text{Pittsburgh } \frac{116 \text{ Hours}}{4015 \text{ Hours}} \times 100 = 2.9\%$$

$$\text{Los Angeles } \frac{136 \text{ Hours}}{2725 \text{ Hours}} \times 100 = 5.0\%$$

Los Angeles, most obviously, is experiencing more than its share of machine repair downtime.

Now let's look at machine repairs:

$$\text{Houston } \frac{253 \text{ Hours}}{8163 \text{ Hours}} \times 100 = 3.1\%$$

$$\text{Pittsburgh } \frac{285 \text{ Hours}}{4015 \text{ Hours}} \times 100 = 7.1\%$$

$$\text{Los Angeles } \frac{312 \text{ Hours}}{2725 \text{ Hours}} \times 100 = 11.4\%$$

Here again, Los Angeles is in far worse shape than Houston and Pittsburgh.

In like fashion, the astute manufacturing manager will use the divisional downtime summary to advantage. Total machine repair hours, for example, constitute almost 27% of all downtime experienced (850 Hours/3199 Hours $\times$ 100 = 26.5%). To the practiced eye, that is quite a bit: Machine repair in most manufacturing operations will probably be among the highest of downtime categories, but it should not amount to 27%. In like fashion, rework is a hefty 746 hours. To a large extent rework can always be reduced and, as a guide, should not exceed 10–15% of downtime hours. In this case it's 23.3% (746 Hours/3199 Hours × 100 = 23.3%) and can readily be reduced.

THE PARETO PRINCIPLE

After carefully analyzing the downtime percentages, the manufacturing manager is then able to more effectively focus the organization's attention on problem correction. Inherent in that statement is the assumption that just a few of the many problems which confront a manufacturing business at any given time generate the lion's share of lost dollars.

If, for example, the manufacturing manager were able to disect the 850 machine repair labor hours lost at PMD during the week, he might find this distribution:

MACHINE REPAIR CATEGORY	DIRECT-LABOR HOURS LOST
Electrical Repairs	574
Mechanical Repairs	105
Hydraulic Repairs	93
Air System Repairs	78
Total:	850 Hours

Electrical repairs are the main problem. If the manufacturing manager had not made this subsequent breakdown, that fact might never have emerged. Having done so, he is in a much better position to take corrective action.

In similar fashion, had he asked *where* the electrical problems were located, these facts might have surfaced:

PLANT	DEPARTMENT	HOURS LOST
Houston	N/C Equipment	160
Pittsburgh	N/C Equipment	94
Los Angeles	N/C Equipment	256
	Total:	510 Hours

Therefore, 510 of the 574 direct labor hours lost to electrical repairs were attributable to problems found in N/C equipment in all three plants.

INTERNATIONAL MACHINERY, INC.
PARTS MANUFACTURING DIVISION
LOS ANGELES PLANT
DOWNTIME ANALYSIS

Week Ending: 8/20

A. SUMMARY	Man-Hours	Percent
Total Direct Labor Hours Worked	2725	100.0%
Direct Labor Hours on Production	1690	62.0%
Direct Labor Hours on Downtime	1035	38.0%

	Direct Labor Man-Hours								
B. DETAIL ANALYSIS	CHUCKERS	GRINDERS	MILLING	DRILLING	HEAT TREAT	PLATE	PAINT	ASSEMBLY	TOTAL
Set-up	42	20	28	46	23	0	5	17	181
Machine adjustments	25	17	11	33	0	9	11	25	131
Rework	56	22	8	27	33	8	21	0	175
Wait-time—materials	0	0	15	0	0	0	0	45	60
Machine repairs	64	38	41	109	18	29	0	13	312
Tooling repairs	27	43	26	20	0	0	0	20	136
Training	0	0	0	0	0	0	0	40	40
Totals:	214	140	129	235	74	46	37	160	1035
Percent of Total:	20.7	13.5	12.5	22.7	7.1	4.4	3.6	15.5	100.0

Figure 6-2. Parts Manufacturing Division: Downtime analysis.

At this stage, the manufacturing manager is in excellent position to focus corrective actions where it will do the most good. The type of analysis this represents is referred to as the "Pareto Principle." Pareto was an Italian economist who discovered early in the twentieth century that a relatively large amount of money was concentrated in a relatively small proportion of the problems that make up the population. The application of the Pareto Principle to manufacturing problems remains a viable tool in the resolution of those problems.

PLANT LEVEL DOWNTIME ANALYSIS

The divisional downtime summary for PMD clearly indicated that something was very wrong at Los Angeles. Since each of the PMD plants prepares their own weekly summary, let's look at the downtime analysis for Los Angeles, displayed in Figure 6-2.

The essential difference between this downtime analysis and the one used at divisional level is that the plant report further analyzes downtime by department. Since we already are aware that much of the Los Angeles downtime problem is concentrated in machine repair, and that much of that is in electrical repairs, the one remaining factor to determine is the departments responsible.

Los Angeles has N/C equipment in its Chucker and Drilling Departments; and as you can see from Figure 6-2, both have a lot of downtime in the machine repair category—64 hours in the Chuckers, and 109 hours in Drilling.

Additionally, Los Angeles has calculated percentages of total downtime attributable to each department, as can be seen at the bottom of Figure 6-2. Notice that the Chuckers and Drilling Departments have between them almost half of all the downtime recorded for all of the departments (20.7% + 22.7% = 43.4%). The finger has been pointed at the primary troubled areas. Effective downtime reductions can now take place.

7
Controlling Output Through Work Measurement

"Production is not the application of tools to materials, but logic to work."
Peter Drucker

One of the most important decisions a manufacturing manager will ever make concerns the selection of the work measurement system he will adopt to control output. Chapters 2 through 5 described various systems which the manufacturing manager can use to control productivity and manpower costs, and Chapter 6 explained how to make use of analytical downtime tools to improve productivity.

Common to all of those subjects is the proper use of a work measurement system to control and improve manufacturing output. Without such a system, output, at best, would be sporadic and generally inconsistent. A work measurement system, tailored to the individual manufacturing organization, is what puts it all together.

TYPES OF WORK MEASUREMENT SYSTEMS

The predicament of the manufacturing manager is this: Which work measurement system should he select? His options are these:

1. No work measurement system
2. Measured daywork
3. Short-interval scheduling

4. Incentive systems
5. Profit sharing plans

1. *No Work Measurement System.* The first option, "No work measurement system," isn't as ridiculous as it may appear to be at first sight. Many manufacturing businesses have operated successfully without application of any work measurement at all, and some will continue to do so in the future.

In a business owned by the workers themselves, (there are quite a few of these companies operating successfully) work measurement is generally not required because all employees are motivated to produce high quantities of output. Obviously, their success is geared to high production quantities and low costs, provided that sales demand remains high. While there is a need for efficient work methods in such organizations, that same need isn't extended to work measurement as a tool to control output.

Manufacturing companies that have low labor content in their products normally have production machinery capable which set the work pace. Automated equipment, for example, where labor is used to load hoppers only, establishes how high production will be. The influence of operators on output for such machinery is minimal. Under this circumstance, work measurement will not pay for itself.

Process machinery, such as that used in chemical plants is another example of a production process that can operate efficiently without the use of a work measurement system. Highly automated, process machinery has a low labor content, and production quantities depend on the capabilities of the equipment rather than its operators.

In other more conventional cases, management may know that work measurement will increase output, but have made a conscious decision not to adopt it since they desire labor peace. In their own minds the cost of work measurement will be far greater than results it brings due to labor-management friction. While such cases are rare, they, nevertheless, do exist; and each management must understand that introduction of a work measurement system in a plant where none has existed before, *will* create labor problems which will be difficult to resolve.

Another factor to be considered is the expense of installing and maintaining a workable and effective work measurement system. Industrial engineers, accountants, personnel people, and a host of others will be required to devote a considerable portion of their working days to the system. Work measurement is not self-perpetuating. It takes a great deal of work and application, not only during the installation phase, but also throughout the life of the program.

In the author's opinion, only 10 to 20% of manufacturing companies can sustain relatively high output without the use of some form of work measurement. In most companies, the conditions described in the preceding paragraphs mostly do not exist. Certainly the typical manufacturing enterprise is not owned by the workers, neither is it strictly composed of automated machinery, nor is labor peace achieved through management's fear of upsetting the union or labor force through introduction of work measurement.

2. *Measured Daywork*. Under measured daywork, work standards are established for production operations, but no financial inducements are offered to operators to meet or exceed those standards. The attainment of work standards is left to the varying abilities—and interests—of individual foremen. With measured daywork skillful foremen can convince operators to meet established standards; other foremen either cannot or will not. If foremen know how to use the standards to increase productivity, and have the support of higher management to enforce the work measurement system, then chances are measured daywork will control and improve production output. That is not usually the case.

Measured daywork can be contrasted to incentive systems on this one basic premise: under incentive systems, production operators are motivated to increase output because their earnings will increase accordingly. Under measured daywork, there is no financial, or other, motivator for operators. Therefore, *measured daywork depends highly on the skills and abilities of individual foremen to make the system successful.* And, as we are all aware, the skills and abilities of individual foremen vary greatly.

Many companies, understanding this premise, attempt to improve the capabilities of their first line supervisors through directed training; that training is structured to achieve consistent application of the measured daywork system throughout the factory. Unfortunately, it seldom succeeds. Measured daywork, to be successful, must involve *all* levels of manufacturing management. While the training can have moderate success with foremen, it rarely goes far enough to involve other organizational layers.

Measured daywork, like many other management systems, can only do the job when each layer of manufacturing management is committed to make the system work. That means use of management reports such as those described in Chapter 2, and the full endorsement and active support of general foremen, plant managers, and the manufacturing manager to take action when standards aren't achieved. Too often, this active involvement of higher management is lacking under measured daywork. Either the follow-up is faulty or the interest isn't sustained. In any case, the results are many times discouraging.

Measured daywork, however, is normally preferable to no work measurement system at all. It has demonstrated its ability, over the years, to increase output in the range of 20 to 60%; but it should be pointed out that many of its successes were attributable, in part, to methods improvements which accompanied the installation of the measured daywork system.

Measured daywork has been most successfully applied to indirect labor functions such as maintenance. Because manufacturing people have generally avoided the onerous task of applying and using work standards for indirect labor, there are usually high labor savings to be gained. Use of a measured daywork system—even a loose one—should result in a fair amount of labor reductions.

Measured daywork will increase direct labor performance when compared with no work measurement at all, but its effectiveness rests largely with the capability of the foremen.

For *most* companies, measured daywork, alone, cannot achieve prodigious increases in output. It must be accompanied by a management control technique which will assume that foremen and managers alike take full advantage of the system.

3. *Short-Interval Scheduling.* SIS is just that technique. SIS combines the best features of a measured daywork system with a proven control technique that sharpens the ability of foremen and managers to increase output.

Chapter 4 explains why, and shows the technique in action.

SIS is measured daywork at its best. It is highly recommended that any major application of measured daywork be implemented through the framework of SIS to achieve maximum savings.

4. *Incentive Systems.* For most production operations, incentive systems appear to offer the best chance for increasing labor performance,

when compared with other work measurement programs. The chief advantage of the incentive system is that it offers financial rewards for operators who achieve output above established work standards. Measured daywork depends on foremen for results; the incentive system drives right to the core—the operator who, through his efforts, determines the success of any work measurement program. Motivating the operator for output is vastly superior to motivating the foreman, simply because the operator will now produce more than he has ever produced before—he is getting paid to do so. Nothing the foreman can offer is quite so potent.

Although money means less today than it did in prior years, most operators will still respond to the inducement to produce more to make more. Since they are on the job anyway, many operators reason that it's probably best to put forth a little more effort to receive a little more cash. In most instances this philosophy tends to dominate their thinking.

Manufacturing organizations whose operators are motivated by incentives tend to produce more output than those companies where measured daywork predominates. A good incentive plan is capable, in most industries, of producing gains up to 25% higher than those produced by a measured daywork system, and up to 15–20% higher than those produced by a plant using short-interval scheduling.

As a rule, the more manual operations there are, the better the chance of incentive systems outproducing any other work measurement system in existence. This is true, particularly if no work measurement system was in effect at all when the incentives were started. When going from a measured daywork system to incentives, productive output will naturally be less because the measured daywork program itself raised output somewhat.

Obviously, in operations where labor content is low and production rates are largely determined by automated machinery, incentive systems will yield but scant gains.

Incentive systems, however, more than other work measurement systems, pose some unique problems which need to be addressed.

First, unions will push hard to negotiate standards. This could possibly nullify a significant portion of the gains management anticipates or is receiving from the incentive system. As time under incentives progresses, that pressure will become stronger; and management will eventually find itself in the position of losing some of the attractive savings previously realized through the incentive plan.

Second, poorly set work standards are hard to remove. Most management-labor contracts prohibit the tightening of work standards without a change in equipment or methods. Therefore, loose standards are perpetuated and cost the company a bundle of money. And regardless of how conscious that management is of this hazard, and regardless of how well prepared it is to confront it, many work standards will be poorly set. Such is the nature of any enormously complex undertaking of which work standards is a perfect example.

Third, while incentive systems are applied essentially to direct labor jobs, how are indirect labor employees motivated? The problem of getting the most work possible from indirect labor is exacerbated when production operators are receiving incentive earnings. Indirect labor employees feel left out, and their morale drops. The trick is to raise their base pay to the point where they feel they are being fairly compensated, but not so much as to induce production operators to bid onto indirect labor jobs whenever they become available. The incentive earnings potential of direct labor *must* exceed base pay rates of indirect labor functions to keep talented and skilled production operators content. That is very difficult to do.

Applying incentive rates to indirect labor jobs is one of the most demanding, if not impossible, tasks to accomplish. The nonrepetitive nature of the typical indirect labor job simply foils the best efforts of management to apply incentives. Indirect labor people will grossly abuse the system, taking shortcuts on the job to achieve incentive earnings, while the quality of their work sharply decreases.

Finally, there are always at play gradual and continuous changes in work methods, processes, equipment, and materials which allow production operators to "beat the system." Over a period of time incentive earnings increase due many times to the ingenuity of production operators. Not that these are bad changes. Certainly, anything that increases production is beneficial. The problem is that operators will hide their improvements so management will be unable to change work standards to accurately reflect working methods. Eventually, operators will restrain production to hide those methods. Incentive earnings will "top out." When that occurs, it becomes inordinately difficult for management to increase productivity without major changes to the production process—and that costs many dollars. In effect, production levels off while costs continue to rise, and management soon finds itself trapped, once again, in the classic cost-benefits spiral. At that stage, management loses. Operators benefit when incentive earnings are max-imized, but company profits deteriorate.

These creeping changes can be countered through rewards to employ-ees for suggesting work improvements. Only in this way can manage-ment hope to offset the gains made from operator ingenuity.

5. *Profit Sharing Plans.* These plans enable all hourly people in man-ufacturing, both direct labor and indirect labor alike, to share the rewards of increased productivity. They are based on plant-wide pro-ductivity improvements. If a plant, for example, had labor content equal to 30% of its cost-of-sales, and known productivity improvements resulted in a reduction of that labor content to 25% of its cost-of-sales, then both management and labor would participate in the profit gain.

The prime advantage of profit sharing plans is that it includes all hourly employees in the plant while management does not have to spend money needed to support an incentive system or measure daywork plan.

The basic detraction from this type of plan is that it does not usually produce output improvements anywhere in the range of incentive sys-tems and, in fact, may not even have the savings potential of an effective measured daywork system. Also, cost savings generated by manage-ment, such as the purchase of new, high production automated equip-ment, must be shared with the labor force. Many managers find this last disadvantage too high a price to pay for profit sharing plans.

Profit sharing plans are also conducive to elevating the voice of labor in management decisions over and above the union-management con-tract. The administration of a profit sharing plan demands the review of essential company matters by both employee representatives and managers. To many managers this is an infringement of their rights simply not to be tolerated.

In summary, listed below are the conditions favoring each type of work measurement system:

No Work Measurement System
1. Worker-owned business.
2. Mostly automated machinery.
3. Low labor content.
4. Strong desire for labor peace (assuming company profitable).
5. Management convinced (often wrongly) that administrative costs of work measurement exceed benefits.

Short-Interval Scheduling
1. High labor content.
2. Company losing money.
3. Large indirect labor force.
4. Measured daywork system in place ineffective (or none being used).

Measured Daywork
1. High labor content.
2. Mostly machine-produced product.
3. Strong, well-trained foremen.
4. Strong interest of upper management.
5. Large indirect labor force.
6. No work measurement system in place currently.

Incentive Systems
1. High labor content.
2. Well-trained industrial engineers.
3. Many manual operations.
4. Strong desire of management for extra production.
5. Expressed desire of union and employees for incentive earnings.

Profit-Sharing Plans
1. Large indirect labor force.
2. Company unwilling to commit resources to support other work measurement systems but needs to increase output.
3. Management-employee-union spirit of cooperation very high.

8
Capacity Analysis and Control

"Nothing is more terrible than activity without insight."

Thomas Carlyle

Chapter 9 and subsequent chapters describe control methods for the traditional materials management functions: production planning and control, inventory management, and purchasing. Chapter 8 shows the manufacturing manager how to determine the capacity of his manufacturing facilities so he can then go on to load them to their fullest.

Every manufacturing manager needs to be aware of what the capacity of his plants are for two reasons. First it assures that realistic workloads are scheduled. Too heavy a workload in relation to capacity leads to missed customer promises and high in-process inventory levels. Too light a workload causes high capacity variances, a cost whose severe negative impact was discussed in Chapter 1.

Manufacturing capacity is the amount of product the facilities are capable of producing within a given time period. Capacity is generally expressed in terms of standard direct labor hours.

It should also be stated that capacity as discussed in this chapter is different than the term "normal capacity" read in Chapter 1. Normal capacity refers to *average* use of the facilities over a number of years while manufacturing capacity as discussed here signifies capability of the facilities to manufacture the most product possible or the most product scheduled.

Generally, capacity is calculated by product line for each production machine in the plant. Using PMD's Los Angeles plant for an example, production capacities will be analyzed. Since Los Angeles is essentially a one-product line plant—stainless steel valves—capacity can be determined by direct calculation of the plant's machinery to generate standard direct labor hours.

Determination of capacity is basically a three-step process:

1. *Determination of Raw Capacity.* This assumes that all machines run seven days per week on three shifts, at eight hours per shift with no allowances for downtime. It is a starting point only and the purpose is to make management aware of the full capability of equipment were it to be employed in its most productive state. Raw capacity is a theoretical number, an ideal or standard to be used when calculating realistic capacities later.

2. *Determination of Planned Capacity.* This calculation is based on the number of days per week the machinery is scheduled to operate along with the number of shifts and the number of hours per shift. It is a step down from raw capacity, but does not yet represent actual capacity available for productive output.

3. *Determination of Available Capacity.* Using planned capacity as a base figure, available capacity realistically subtracts standard hours lost because of downtime and yields. Yields include direct labor hours for producing both avoidable and unavoidable scrap. Unavoidable scrap examples are chips and shavings removed during machining operations, skeleton scrap from stamping operations, and gates end risers out from castings.

In the example that follows, Los Angeles calculated *weekly* capacity numbers. In actual practice monthly or annual numbers can be used; the difference is a matter of convenience.

Step 1—Raw Capacity. Figure 8-1 illustrates how PMD's Los Angeles plant computes raw capacity. The left-hand column lists all of Los Angeles' productive departments which generate standard direct labor hours. The next column shows how many production machines there are in each department.

The third column, "Crew Size" represents the number of machines operators per machine. Drills, for example, have a crew size of one man (or woman) per machine. The number .5 shown opposite both chuckers and grinders means that one operator runs two machines; hence the .5 (one-half) operator per machine.

The next column, "Total Crew" is derived by multiplying the available machines by their crew sizes. There are 12 chuckers, for example,

INTERNATIONAL MACHINERY INC.
PARTS MANUFACTURING DIVISION
CAPACITY ANALYSIS
STEP # 1
DETERMINATION OF WEEKLY RAW CAPACITY

PLANT: LOS ANGELES

DEPARTMENT	AVAILABLE MACHINES	CREW SIZE	TOTAL CREW	×	DAYS AVAILABLE	×	SHIFTS PER DAY	×	HOURS PER SHIFT	=	RAW CAPACITY STANDARD DIRECT LABOR HOURS
Chuckers	12	.5	6		7		3		8		1008
Grinders	10	.5	5		7		3		8		840
Millers	10	1.0	10		7		3		8		1680
Drills	10	1.0	10		7		3		8		1680
Heat treat	2	.5	1		7		3		8		168
Plating line	2	1.0	2		7		3		8		336
Paint booths	3	1.0	3		7		3		8		504
Assembly lines	2	4.0	8		7		3		8		1344
Total Plant:			45								7560

Figure 8-1. Parts Manufacturing Division: Capacity analysis. Step # 1 Determination of weekly raw capacity.

and crew size is .5. Therefore: 12 chuckers × .5 crew size = 6 operators. Notice that, if all production machines at Los Angeles are fully staffed, there would be 45 direct labor operators needed per shift (See bottom of "Total Crew" column).

"Days Available" is seven. When raw capacity is being determined, Saturdays and Sundays are always included in the calculations.

In like fashion, when computing raw capacity, three shifts per day and eight hours per day are always used as seen in the columns "Shifts Per Day" and "Hours Per Shift."

The last column, "Raw Capacity-Standard Direct Labor Hours" reflects total hours available during the week. It is derived as seen here:

$$\frac{\text{Total}}{\text{Crew}} \times \frac{\text{Days}}{\text{Available}} \times \frac{\text{Shifts}}{\text{Per Day}} \times \frac{\text{Hours}}{\text{Per Shift}} = \text{Raw Capacity}$$

Totaling raw capacity numbers for all production departments at Los Angeles, there are 7560 standard direct labor hours available per week if *all* productive equipment were operated *all* of the time without *any* delays. Obviously, this number is a jumping-off point only. It is theo-

INTERNATIONAL MACHINERY INC.
PARTS MANUFACTURING DIVISION
CAPACITY ANALYSIS
STEP # 2
DETERMINATION OF WEEKLY PLANNED CAPACITY

PLANT: LOS ANGELES

DEPARTMENT	AVAILABLE MACHINES	PLANNED MACHINES	TOTAL CREW	×	DAYS PLANNED	×	SHIFTS PLANNED	×	HOURS PER SHIFT	=	PLANNED CAPACITY STANDARD DIRECT LABOR HOURS
Chuckers	12	10	5		5		1		10		250
Grinders	10	10	5		5		1		10		250
Millers	10	8	8		5		1		10		400
Drills	10	8	8		5		1		10		400
Heat treat	2	2	1		5		1		10		50
Plating line	2	2	2		5		1		10		100
Paint booths	3	3	3		5		1		10		150
Assembly lines	2	2	8		5		1		10		400
Total Plant:			40								2000

Figure 8-2. Parts Manufacturing Division:Capacity analysis. Step # 2 Determination of weekly planned capacity.

retical, but forms the base for calculating planned capacity, discussed next.

Step 2—Planned Capacity. Figure 8-2 describes the second step used in calculating factory capacity. It is termed "Planned Capacity" and reflects the number of days per week, shifts per day, and hours per shift actually planned by management.

All of the columns, except one, are the same for Figure 8-2 as they were for Figure 8-1. The exception is the third column titled, "Planned Machines." That column shows the number of production machines Los Angeles management plans on running. The chuckers, for example, have 12 available machines, but management will run only 10. That is not unusual. Two machines are planned as spares should another chucker (or a production machine in another department) become unavailable because of repairs or lack of material.

Using the "Crew Size" column of Figure 8-1, the "Total Crew" is then determined based on planned machines to be run. ("Crew Size" is multiplied by "Planned Machines").

From there on out, the calculations for Figure 8-2 are the same as for Figure 8-1. The product of "Total Crew," "Days Planned," "Shifts Planned," and "Hours Per Shift" result in the planned capacity in standard direct labor hours seen in the right-hand column.

Because Los Angeles is a new plant, management has decided to operate one shift, ten hours per shift until initial production problems are resolved. Also, extra capacity was planned for Los Angeles to provide for growth. Consequently, only one shift is currently in use. PMD management anticipates a full two shifts within a year to eighteen months.

Total planned capacity, therefore, is only 2000 standard direct labor hours weekly. Contrast that to the 7560 standard direct labor hours of raw capacity as shown in Figure 8-1 and it is plain to see that Los Angeles has much room for growth.

Step 3—Available Capacity. Planned capacity is still one step short of actual capacity. Available capacity will provide the final number. Available capacity is planned capacity less reserves for downtime and yields.

Downtime is composed of such production delays as machine repairs, inspection time, and material shortages. It does *not* include nonutilization of machinery as cited in the chuckers where only 10 of the department's 12 chuckers were scheduled to be run.

In the calculation of available capacity the inversion of downtime is used and it is called "Uptime." Uptime is the amount of time production machinery is in operation less allowances for known downtime. If, for example, it has been found that downtime for grinding machines has been 25%, its uptime is 75%.

Uptime is always a *planned* number. Should management feel that downtime for grinding machines can be reduced to 20%, then it will plan an uptime of 80% in its calculation of available capacity.

Yields, the other reserve in available capacity, reflects standard direct labor hours lost for avoidable scrap (mistakes) plus unavoidable scrap previously described.

Figure 8-3 shows how to determine available capacity. As usual, the left-hand column lists Los Angeles' production departments. The next column lists planned standard hours taken from Figure 8-2.

Planned standard hours are then multiplied by the uptime objective

INTERNATIONAL MACHINERY INC.
PARTS MANUFACTURING DIVISION
CAPACITY ANALYSIS
STEP # 3
DETERMINATION OF WEEKLY AVAILABLE CAPACITY

PLANT: LOS ANGELES

DEPARTMENT	PLANNED STANDARD HOURS		UPTIME OBJECTIVE PERCENT		YIELD PERCENT		AVAILABLE CAPACITY STANDARD DIRECT LABOR HOURS
Chuckers	250	×	70	×	90	=	158
Grinders	250		80		90		180
Millers	400		80		90		288
Drills	400		75		95		285
Heat treat	50		90		98		44
Plating line	100		90		97		87
Paint booths	150		95		97		138
Assembly lines	400		80		95		304
Total Plant:	2000						1484

Figure 8-3. Parts Manufacturing Division: Capacity analysis. Step # 3 Determination of weekly available capapcity.

as a percentage and the resulting number is multiplied by the yield percentage. (Yield is based on historical averages). The final result is available capacity expressed as standard direct labor hours. For Los Angeles, that number is 1484 standard direct labor hours.

CAPACITY SUMMARY

It is helpful at this stage to put raw capacity, planned capacity, and available capacity, together and compare them as shown in Figure 8-4.

The first and most obvious conclusion is that available capacity of 1484 standard hours is but a small percentage of the 7560 standard hours of raw capacity. That is true, but it must be remembered that Los Angeles is a new plant and that available capacity will expand to more closely approximate raw capacity given time. Shifts will be added to increase available capacity. Additionally, as time progresses and the learning curve extends, uptime and yields will improve as management and operators refine production operations.

INTERNATIONAL MACHINERY INC.
PARTS MANUFACTURING DIVISION
CAPACITY ANALYSIS
SUMMARY

PLANT: LOS ANGELES

| | STANDARD DIRECT LABOR HOURS—WEEKLY | | |
DEPARTMENT	RAW CAPACITY	PLANNED CAPACITY	AVAILABLE CAPACITY
Chuckers	1008	250	158
Grinders	840	250	180
Millers	1680	400	288
Drills	1680	400	285
Heat treat	168	50	44
Plating line	336	100	87
Paint booths	504	150	138
Assembly lines	1344	400	304
Total Plant:	7560	2000	1484

Note: Planned capacity is based on one shift, five days per week, ten hours per day.

Figure 8-4. Parts Manufacturing Division: Capacity analysis summary.

Capacity planning allows manufacturing management to marry production forecasts with available capacity. Through knowledge of what plant capacity is, management can more effectively make plans for future workloads. As sales levels grow, manufacturing management will have a base upon which to ask for additional facilities.

9
Production Planning and Control: Cycle Forecasting

"Facts are nothing until brought into connection with some general law."
Louis Agassiz

Production planning and control is the very essence of a manufacturing organization. The purchase and use of materials, the movement and control of parts in manufacturing, the warehousing and shipment of products to customers, these activities constitute the basic determinants of success in manufacturing. An effective production planning and control function enables a manufacturing organization to meet customer delivery requirements, maintain low inventories, and minimize production costs. And the core activity of production planning and control is forecasting.

Forecasting determines how much material will be purchased, stored, and manufactured, how large inventories will be, how well customer delivery commitments will be met, and how many people will be employed in manufacturing. Forecasting of orders is the first activity of the production planning and control system, and its success—or lack of it—has made or broken the careers of many manufacturing managers.

The most established procedure used to forecast orders is the weekly or monthly meeting between sales and manufacturing managers. It is usually at these meetings that forecasts are made based on sales expectations.

The problem with this method is universal; sales managers—invariably optimistic and concerned about satisfying customer commitments for fast delivery, almost always project greater sales levels than those which actually occur. They reason that an optimistic outlook on sales will keep the factories producing at high enough levels to satisfy the requirements of an avalanche of customers.

Of course, when the anticipated avalanche turns into a small trickle, the person holding the bag won't be the sales manager. Inevitably, the person who will be blamed for high inventories and overmanned shifts will be the manufacturing manager. Regardless of fancy platitudes issued from above concerning the responsibility of sales for issuing realistic forecasts, it will *always* be the job of manufacturing management to hold down inventory and manpower costs in relation to sales. Unfair as that might be, that's the way it really is! So it behooves every manufacturing manager to learn how to forecast realistically. One such method, and one I've come to admire for its relative precision, is called cycle forecasting.

CYCLE FORECASTING

Cycle forecasting, a technique developed almost 25 years ago by the Institute For Trend Research, recognizes that there will almost always be peaks and troughs in business orders, and that those peaks and troughs can be roughly predicted. Regardless of product or technology, cycles occur, and they appear to occur within all economic and political institutions.

Cycle forecasting predicts when those orders will expand and when they will contract. It is based on the fact that, throughout economic history, cycles have been artificially induced by businesspeople and consumers, through either their optimism or pessimism regarding the prevailing economic climate. Cycles occur, in other words, when people defer purchases because of fear, and later make those same purchases because of their belief that business conditions are improving.

PMD's Houston plant has been using cycle forecasting for many years to predict inventory and manpower requirements. They start by listing actual monthly order rates in dollars for the past several years, as seen in the first column of Figure 9-1. The next column, "Moving Annual Total" shows the current twelve-month total. As these numbers

INTERNATIONAL MACHINERY, INC.
PARTS MANUFACTURING DIVISION
CYCLE FORECASTING CALCULATIONS

	ORDERS*	MOVING ANNUAL TOTAL*	ORDER LEVEL %	
1979 J	1.13			Note: All numbers marked
F	1.42			* expressed as millions of
M	1.66			dollars.
A	1.46			
M	1.50			
J	1.68			
J	1.58			
A	1.39			
S	1.66			
O	1.57			
N	1.64			
D	1.81	18.50		
1980 J	1.85	19.22		
F	2.03	19.83		
M	2.49	20.66		
A	2.06	21.26		
M	2.03	21.79		
J	2.11	22.22		
J	1.94	22.58		
A	1.91	23.10		
S	1.95	23.39		
O	2.44	24.26		
N	2.12	24.74		
D	2.50	25.43		
1981 J	1.88	25.46	132.5%	
F	2.59	26.02	131.2	
M	3.14	26.67	129.1	
A	2.91	27.52	129.4	
M	2.87	28.36	130.2	
J	2.95	29.20	131.4	
J	2.62	29.88	132.3	
A	2.60	30.57	132.3	
S	3.45	32.07	137.1	
O	2.90	32.53	134.1	
N	3.40	33.81	136.7	
D	3.38	34.69	136.4	

Figure 9-1. Parts Manufacturing Division: Cycle forecasting calculations.

are accumulated the total for current month is added and the total for the same month during last year is dropped. The moving annual total for January, 1980, for example, was calculated this way:

Total for 19/79:	$18.50 Million
Plus 1/80 Orders:	1.85 Million
Sub-Total:	$20.35 Million
Less 1/79 Orders:	1.13 Million
Moving Annual Total—1/80:	$19.22 Million

Finally, each current moving annual total is divided by the year-ago moving annual total to derive the next column, "Order Level," as shown here for January, 1981:

$$1/81 \text{ Order Level} = \frac{1/81 \text{ Moving Annual Total}}{1/80 \text{ Moving Annual Total}}$$

$$1/81 \text{ Order Level} = \frac{\$25.46 \text{ Million}}{\$19.22 \text{ Million}} \times 100 = 132.5\%$$

The order level tends to reduce the impact of seasonal variations and other factors affecting incoming orders such as order processing delays. The resultant order level trend clearly illustrates basic changes in the ordering cycle alone.

Compare actual orders for 1981 with their corresponding order levels for the same months to see the differences. April and May, for example, show actual declines in the number of orders received while their corresponding order levels are steadily increasing, signaling an upturn in the order cycle. This trend is verified by the higher number of actual orders received from September through December.

If Houston had reduced its purchasing and manpower levels based on decreasing incoming orders experienced in April and May, the plant would have been in poor position to handle the larger influx of orders six months later. They conceivably could have failed to honor customer commitments, or they might have been forced to extend customer delivery dates while they built-up inventories and hired and trained additions to the workforce.

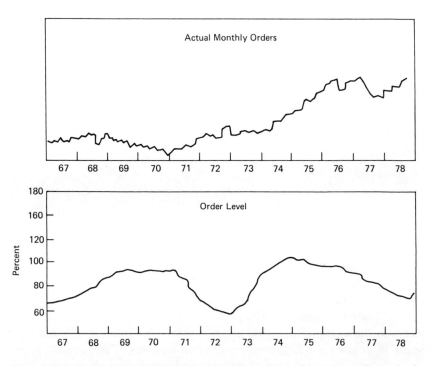

Figure 9-2. Parts Manufacturing Division, Houston Plant: Comparison of open orders and order levels.

Figure 9-2 graphs actual new orders vs. order levels for Houston during the period 1967–1978. Notice the major differences between the graphs. Quite obviously, looking at actual new orders alone is not enough to discern sales trends. Cycle forecasting has helped Houston prepare for major shifts in the marketplace. Its plant manager has been able to match inventory and manpower levels with long-term market needs.

THE BUSINESS CYCLE

Cycle forecasting is predicated upon the inevitability of peaks and valleys in the business cycle. As shown in Figure 9-3, there are six distinct phases, each recognizable, and each possessing its own unique characteristics:

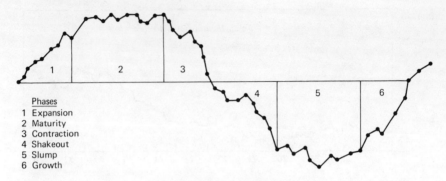

Figure 9-3. The business cycle.

1. Expansion. This phase occurs during a period of optimism. It is recognizable by gains in employment, business increases, and a rapidly improving gross national product. Productivity increases and purchasing agents contract for additional orders.

2. Maturity. The end of the expansion period is marked by narrower gains on the chart for a period of approximately three months and most gains thereafter are balanced by some downturns. The curve "flattens out." During this period employment and business activity remain high, demand triggers inflationary price increases, and plants are near full capacity.

3. Contraction. Three consecutive months of decline on the chart mark the start of a period of business contraction. Purchasing levels drop-off slightly, inventories increase, plants stop hiring people, overtime is drastically reduced, and businesses curtail capital improvement plans. Business, though, continues to be good but not at the level of the preceding period.

4. Shakeout. When the order level drops below 100 and subsequent points on the chart continue to fall the business cycle has reached its shakeout period. This phase is recognizable by plant layoffs, sales declines, inventory reductions, decreases in the prime rate, and a general sense of pessimism. Business plans are generally curtailed and unemployment levels begin climbing.

5. Slump. This is the roughest period of all; if business conditions are severe enough a depression ensues. Plant layoffs continue, employment rates begin to alarm the politicians, capital improvement plans are virturally nonexistent, and inventories continue to climb to discouraging levels.

6. Growth. Usually three successive points of growth on the chart signal the faint beginnings of a period of economic growth and recovery. Plant layoffs stop and some companies begin to slowly rehire skilled employees. Purchasing agents see the first glimmer of hope through small increases in buying levels. Inventories begin to decline and business makes new capital improvement plans. The GNP begins to rise.

A normal business cycle lasts about four years with two-and-one-half years above the order level of 100, and about one-and-one-half years below 100. Obviously, the duration of a business cycle is influenced by a great many variables such as whether the country is at war or peace, the strength of the dollar both home and abroad, the type of product being manufactured, and literally dozens of other factors. *The business cycle curve, therefore, must be individually interpreted by each company using its own product demand and in the context of its own situation.*

USE OF THE BUSINESS CYCLE

The manufacturing manager can use the business cycle curve described in Figure 9-3 to plan ahead. Listed below are typical actions which can be taken by the manufacturing manager during each of the six phases of the business cycle:

1. Expansion.

Build or expand manufacturing facilities.
Install new machine tools.
Expand the labor force.
Build inventory.
Subcontract work.
Write-off obsolete inventory losses.
Develop new vendors.
Start training programs.

2. Maturity.

Sell surplus machinery.
Maintain—but not increase—inventories.

Freeze all expansion plans.
Freeze salaried hiring.
Develop plans for business downturn.
Plan to reduce subcontract work.
Get machinery in top condition.
Work overtime.

3. *Contraction.*

Begin layoffs.
Start reducing inventories.
Stop training programs.
Reduce purchasing levels.
Establish tight budgets.
Avoid long-term purchasing contracts.
Reduce fixed costs wherever possible.
Begin cost reduction program.
Stop all overtime.

4. *Shakeout.*

Continue layoffs.
Continue reducing inventories.
Reduce purchasing levels further.
Freeze capital improvement programs.
Get tougher on customer returns.
Reduce indirect labor activities.
Reduce management deadwood.
Combine functions.

5. *Slump.*

Stop layoffs. Hold onto skilled people.
Consider eliminating a shift.
Set tighter budgets.
Make new expansion plans.
Begin purchasing capital equipment.
Keep cost reduction programs moving.
Locate better vendors.

6. *Growth.*

Begin rehiring skilled employees.
Build inventories.
Move ahead with expansion plans.
Place added purchasing orders.
Prepare training programs.
Hire new salaried employees.
Introduce new products.

10
Production Planning and Control: Scheduling

"The pace of events is moving so fast that unless we can find some way to keep our sights on tomorrow, we cannot expect to be in touch with today."

Dean Rusk

If forecasting is the first essential step of effective production planning and control, then scheduling—the drafting of the production plan—is the second essential step. Scheduling takes the information from the forecast and changes it to specific planning for shop operations.

The objective of scheduling is to plan factory operations to meet customer delivery dates and to do so with commitment of a minimum of inventory at the lowest possible operating costs. Poor scheduling results in either low inventory and missed customer delivery promises or high inventory and high operating costs. An effective scheduling system falls somewhere between those two conditions and optimizes resources.

A comprehensive scheduling system has these factors in common:

1. Anybody can understand it and work with it. Its simplicity is proved through its usage.

2. It establishes obtainable goals. Those goals are neither too loose nor too tight. The schedule provides time to respond to the unexpected—a common and anticipated problem in *all* manufacturing operations.

3. It provides reliable information to users. Manufacturing people can depend on its accuracy and use the information to make decisions regarding changes in the schedule in response to problems as they arise.

4. Deviations to the schedule are highlighted in time for responsible supervisors to make needed changes. Since deviations are the prime reason for failure to achieve schedules, they must come to the immediate attention of supervisors as soon as they occur. Time is always critical.

5. It must be flexible enough to allow for changes to be made without disrupting the schedule itself.

THE ELEMENTS OF SCHEDULING

All scheduling systems have certain elements in common. Whether the production planning system is done manually or by computer makes no difference; all scheduling systems must consist of:

A. The machines and other work centers to be scheduled.
B. The routing of parts through manufacturing.
C. The length of time it takes to manufacture and assemble the product (lead time).

Let's examine each of these in somewhat more detail.

AREAS TO BE SCHEDULED

For each individual machine or assembly operation, a schedule must be developed for every different part they handle which identifies:

Machine number.
Part number of product being manufactured.
Standard hours to produce the part.

Houston, for example, has a master schedule of its two heat treat furnaces which shows the following information:

| | | PART NUMBERS | | |
| | WEEKLY* AVAILABLE | 500 PCS | 270 PCS | 160 PCS |
MACHINE NUMBER	CAPACITY	PMD 1-263	264-495	496-1007
H.T.-1	72 hours	1.0 hours	1.8 hours	2.2 hours
H.T.-2	70 hours	1.1 hours	1.9 hours	2.4 hours

*Refer to Chapter 8 for a discussion of the derivation of available capacity.

The first heat treat furnace, H.T.-1, operating two shifts, five days per week, is available for a weekly load of 72 hours while the other heat treat furnace, H.T.-2, has shown an historical availability of 70 hours per week. Under "Part Numbers," the number of pieces and heat treat times are listed by part number groups. Above those numbers is the maximum quantity which can be heat-treated at one time. If, for example, Houston schedules 250 pieces of part number PMD-6 and 250 pieces of PMD-204 to be heat treated, they will be loaded into the furnace together and will take 1.0 hours to process in H.T.-1 or 1.1 hours in H.T.-2.

Using this chart, the scheduler can then fully load the heat treat furnaces to the extent of their available capacity.

In similar fashion, the master scheduling system keeps cards (or computer files) for each part number and operation in the plant.

ROUTINGS

While the master schedule identifies work to be done at individual machines, routings describe the flow of parts through the shop. A routing is in essence, the road map of the parts being manufactured in the plant. A routing will describe the operation to be performed, the machines and assembly lines where they will be performed, and the standard hours needed to complete the schedule at individual work stations.

A typical routing for manufacture of a 3.5″ line coupling is shown in Figure 10-1, Houston's routing for that part.

The top of the routing describes order data: part name and number, customer, quantity, and delivery date.

The bottom of the routing shows department, operation number (the cost center of the operation), the operation to be performed, standard hours per piece, total standard hours, and comments. Set-up times are factored into the standrds.

For the operations heat treat, assembly, and pack, the comments display 500, 250, and 1000 pieces respectively. Those numbers are related to the standard hours/piece, heat treat, for example, shows 1.0 standard hours needed to process 500 pieces. For 2500 pieces the total is five standard hours:

$$\left(\frac{2500 \text{ pieces}}{500 \text{ pieces} / \text{hour}} \right)$$

ROUTING TICKET   Houston

Part: 3.5″ Line Coupling   *Part Number:* PMD—37
Lot Number: 2066   *Customer:* Richards Supply, Galveston
Quantity: 2500   *Delivery Date:* 4/18/81

DEPARTMENT	OPERATION	OPERATION NUMBER	STD.HOURS PER PIECE	TOTAL STD. HOURS	COMMENTS
Stocking	Stock	106	—	.2	
Saws	Cut to size	219	.05	125.0	
Boring mills	Taper bore	305	.03	75.0	
Chuckers	Chamfer and tap	412	.01	25.0	
Heat treat −1	Temper	533	1.00	5.0	500 pcs.
Assembly	Assemble caps	640	1.00	10.0	250 pcs.
Pack	Carton parts	718	3.00	7.5	1000 pcs.

SPECIAL INSTRUCTIONS: USE MASTER CARTONS WITH TYPE # 3 CORRU-
GATED SEPARATORS. SHIP ON TRUCK # 2 DESTI-
NATION GALVESTON.

Figure 10-1. Parts Manufacturing Division, Houston Plant: Routing ticket.

LEAD TIMES

This is not simply a matter of adding standard hours from routings to determine how long it takes parts to travel through the plant.

Lead times must include *all* time spent in the plant, and not only time spent in operations. Normally, the disparity is amazing. Time spent during machining or assembly is termed "In-Process Time" as contrasted to time spent waiting (for any number of reasons) which is called "Total Process Time."

Houston decided to identify total process time vs. in-process time to establish realistic lead times for meeting customer commitments. That was done by flagging a group of orders going through the plant. Times of arrival and departure for each order were recorded on a work ticket for each operation. Since standard hours had been determined for each part and operation, Houston management already knew in-process time. Using the work tickets, they were then fortified with total process time.

A chart was drawn (Figure 10-2) illustrating the relationship. The sequence of operations is listed on the left side of the chart. The next columns describe in-process time, total process time, and idle time.

From this a formula can be expressed:

Total Process Time = In-Process Time + Idle Time.

From Figure 10-2 the small number of in-process hours—247.7—is in sharp contrast with idle time of 493.4 hours. This is not unusual. In fact, in many operations, idle time constitutes up to 90% of total process time compared with 67% seen in Figure 10-2 $\left(\dfrac{493.4 \text{ hrs.}}{741.1 \text{ hrs.}} \right)$

Lead time, then, is comprised of several elements. These are:

Operation time (Machining, assembly, etc.)
Setup time
Queue time (Waiting to be worked)
Delay time (Machine problems, etc.)
Wait time (Finished operation. Waiting to be moved to next operation.)
Transit time

Determination of lead times must take all of the elements described above into account to be realistic.

TOTAL PROCESS TIME vs. IN-PROCESS TIME

Product: 3.5" line cplg.   Quantity: 2500   Lot Number: 2066

| | HOURS | | |
OPERATION	IN-PROCESS TIME	TOTAL PROCESS TIME	IDLE TIME
Stock	.2	26.4	26.2
Saw	125.0	175.5	50.5
Bore	75.0	128.6	53.6
Chuck	25.0	78.8	53.8
Heat-treat	5.0	143.2	138.2
Assemble	10.0	63.5	53.5
Pack	7.5	125.1	117.6
Total	247.7	741.1	493.4

Figure 10-2. Parts Manufacturing Division, Houston Plant: Lead time analysis.

REVERSE LOADING

Most production planning systems load the plants from front to rear. Loading is accomplished by scheduling each subsequent plant operation. Inevitably, this practice swells total process time.

Reverse loading reduces total process time. This happens through scheduling the last operation first, and then loading all prior operations in reverse sequence. Let's observe reverse loading at work in PMD's Houston plant.

At one time Houston scheduled all of its operations from front to back. A typical operation was production of ½″ standard couplings. Total process time for 1000 of these couplings averaged eight shifts. They could be sized and shaped on screw machines in one shift, and finished on chuckers in four shifts. Chamfering and tapping would average two shifts. The final steps, plating and packing were accomplished in one shift. Several thousand couplings jammed the manufacturing process during the eight-shift span, and delivery dates were constantly missed.

Houston management found two major problems upon analyzing the production planning and control system. First, all orders were loaded from beginning operations, and second, all order were processed in discrete lots. Before a lot could move from one operation to another, every piece of that particular order had to first be completed. This factor alone created large gaps in the work flow. Large lots would take days to process, and subsequent departments would not start work on them until every last piece was completed in the prior operation. Because of this practice, labor efficiencies suffered and missed customer delivery dates were the order of the day. The 1000 pieces of ½″ standard couplings moved through manufacturing like this:

PIECES PROCESSED	OPERATION	TIME TO PROCESS
1000	Screw machines	8 Hours Monday
1000	Chuckers	32 Hours Tuesday–Friday
1000	Chamfers and taps	16 Hours Monday–Tuesday
1000	Plating line	2 Hours Wednesday
1000	Packing	6 Hours Wednesday

Reverse loading was started to reduce the total process time and lot tickets were printed to allow movement of partial orders between departments. The two changes reduced total process time (lead time) from eight to five shifts:

PIECES PROCESSED	OPERATION	TIME TO PROCESS
1000.	Screw machines	Monday
1000	Chuckers	Monday–Thursday
1000	Chamfers and taps	Tuesday–Thursday
1000	Plating line	Friday
1000	Packing	Friday

THE PRODUCTION PLAN

The scheduling activities described thus far have been directed at movements between departments and throughout the entire plant as a whole. When scheduling within a given department, however, another tool needs to be developed to schedule parts on the many machines each department has. That tool is called the "Production Plan."

Figure 10-3 is the production plan for Houston's Grinding Department. The left side of the plan shows work scheduled to be run in the Grinding Department the week of April 14, 1980. It details lot number, product, tooling number for that order, quantity ordered, and pieces per hour required by established work standards for the lot's product.

PMD HOUSTON PLANT PRODUCTION PLAN				GRINDING MACHINES												WK. ENDING 4/14/80	
MACHINE HOURS AVAILABLE (TWO SHIFTS)																		
				60	60	60	60	60	60	60	60	60	60	60	60		TOTAL DEPT.
LOT NO.	PRODUCT	TOOLING NO.	QUANTITY	PIECES PER HOUR	1	2	3	4	5	6	7	8	9	10	11	12	
2135	6″ Studs	A143Z	4000	100	40												40
2243	1″ Cplgs.	A443T	30000	300	20	60	20										100
2692	½″ Plugs	A672V	100000	400			40	60	60	60	30						250
2204	5″ Liners	A152R	25000	125							30	60	60	50			200
2725	8″ Studs	A142N	4000	80										10	40		50
																Open	0
TOTAL SCHEDULED MAN-HOURS:					60	60	60	60	60	60	60	60	60	60	40	0	640

Figure 10-3. Parts Manufacturing Division, Houston Plant: Production plan.

The right side of the plan lists all twelve grinding machines available for use as well as the available hours for each machine during the week. Available capacity for the grinders on a two-shift basis has been calculated to be 60 hours.

Underneath each machine, scheduled hours are listed based on the particular lot to be run. The first lot, 2135, calls for a run of 4000 pieces; at a standard of 100 pieces per hour there are 40 hours needed to complete the lot $\left(\dfrac{4000 \text{ pieces}}{100 \text{ pieces per hour}} \right)$. Scheduled hours for each lot are calculated in the same manner, and each grinder is then loaded to its capacity of 60 hours.

When scheduled loads exceed individual machine capacity, additional machines are added. Lot 2243, for example, needs 100 hours to run the needed 30,000 pieces $\left(\dfrac{30,000 \text{ pieces}}{300 \text{ pieces per hour}} \right)$. Since grinder #1 has only 40 of its available 60 hours scheduled, 20 hours of lot 2243 are added to grinder #1, then 60 hours to grinder #2, and the residue, 20 hours, to grinder #3.

The far right-hand column contains total scheduled machine hours (in this case machine-hours are equivalent to man-hours) by lot number and for the entire department.

The production plan is projected weekly for the following week. Normally it is made on Wednesday or Thursday. By scheduling work ahead of time, management is in control of its own fate; any problems anticipated during preparation of the schedule can be handled before the schedule is implemented. This saves time and keeps costs down.

The production plan offers additional advantages:

Departmental workloads and individual machine workloads are readily observable.

Scheduled machine hours are planned ahead and are clearly depicted.

Scheduled machine hours are measured against capacity.

Work standards are listed for use by manufacturing foremen.

The production plan can be stepped-down daily schedule segments for control by foremen.

Machine overloads as well as underutilized machines are made apparent so the schedule can be altered accordingly.

MATERIALS REQUIREMENTS PLANNING

When a company manufactures a complex piece of machinery such as a tractor or machine tool, material requirements planning (MRP) can sometimes save it many dollars through regulation of the production planning and control system. MRP is a computerized production and inventory control system aimed at reducing inventory levels, improving customer delivery schedules, and properly utilizing plant capacity.

MRP uses the principle of reverse loading mentioned earlier. It plans quantities to be delivered to the assembly lines at given dates. Working backwards in the manufacturing process it then indicates quantities of parts needed in manufacturing to support the assembly schedule, and then goes on to specify purchasing quantities, all within a time framework. When shortages and delays occur, the MRP system adjusts production schedules to meet the new requirements.

MRP answers the following questions:

What parts should be built?
How many parts should be built?
When should the parts be ready?

MRP starts just like any other production planning and control system, computerized or manual, with the forecast of product needed to satisfy customer demands. (A unique method of forecasting was described in Chapter 9, Cycle Forecasting.)

Next, the bill of materials is used. A bill of materials lists all of the parts and components of a product, as well as its assemblies. The MRP "explodes" the bill of materials into the many thousands of parts needed to meet schedules. The bill of materials, then, is the base document which "tells" the MRP what to build.

One of the real world values of MRP is seen during periods of change and uncertainty. If, for example, production increases 20% over forecast, or if there is a dramatic change in the product mix, MRP provides the information needed to adjust the production cycle and inventory. The MRP system will indicate what parts must be ordered, the number of standard hours needed, how many shifts will be necessary, and other data aimed at changing the schedule in the most efficient manner.

MRP is a subject by itself that can easily fill a book this size. *It is also a system demanding the greatest of skills in its implementation. It should never be installed by anybody without relevant knowledge of MRP systems.* The manufacturing manager considering an MRP system should consult an MRP expert before committing his company (and his reputation) to MRP. MRP is a proven tool in the production planning and control toolkit, but it is a sensitive and expensive tool, indeed. Use it with caution.

11
Production Planning and Control: Priority Control

"A man who dares to waste one hour of time has not discovered the value of life."

Charles Darwin

Forecasting and scheduling are the first two essential components of production planning and control. The third component is control-control to assure the schedule is being obtained, that inventories are adequate throughout manufacturing, that operators are achieving at standard production rates, that subassemblies are ready at the right time to achieve final assembly schedules, and that parts are being purchased in accordance with the production plan.

One of the better control instruments at the command of production planning and control people is called "Priority Control." Priority control is a procedure which helps decide the status of orders in manufacturing and indicates which orders should be worked first. It establishes work priorities and helps production planning people decide which orders to review for rescheduling or even cancellation.

Priority control can be used with either manual or computerized scheduling systems, but is easier and less expensive to use in computerized form. Often it is associated with MRP programs. Under MRP, forecasted and firm requirements for purchased parts, raw materials, and manufactured parts are scheduled by month into the future (usually twelve months). Orders for both purchased and manufactured parts are then prepared based on dates needed as determined from the MRP program. At this stage the priority control program takes over. It adjusts schedules, production plans, and purchase order deliveries for changes in the requirements of purchased parts, raw materials or manufactured parts.

Requirements are constantly changing. This is a characteristic all production planning and control people know they must face. Customers cancel or modify orders all the time. This continual shuffling of orders changes the requirements. Some parts may need to be advanced in the schedule while other parts must be cancelled. To keep inventories current, all schedules for both purchased and manufactured parts must now be adjusted.

When Houston's production plans are revised, a new MRP computer run changes time-phased requirements. Using the master MRP file (which lists all customers' orders) the priority of each order is calculated based on this information:

1. Lead time by operation.
2. Date order is needed.
3. Standard hours by operation.

The measurement used in priority control is based on that information (shown above) to obtain the following ratio:

$$\text{Priority ratio} = \frac{\text{Number of days till needed.}}{\text{Number of days work to be done.}}$$

An example of Houston's priority control ratio for 5″ liners for part number PMD-62 follows:

Part PMD-62 has the following customer parts requirements for the first quarter of 1981:

	JAN.	FEB.	MARCH
Assemblies	3000	3000	2000
Service Parts	2000	0	4000

The MRP system shows the following inventory balances for PMD-62:

	JAN.	FEB.	MARCH
Beginning Balance:	8000	3000	0
Less: Requirements*	5000	3000	6000
Ending Balance	3000	0	6000

PMD-62 for January shows 8,000 available parts which will be depleted the end of February. There is an open order in manufacturing for 10,000 pieces which needs to be completed by March 1 to meet the requirements for parts. The priority ratio for this order would be calculated as follows:

The number of days till needed extends from January 1 to March 1, a period of 42 work (not calendar) days. This number is the numerator of the priority ratio.

The denominator, number of days work to be done, is 65 (Houston's lead time on each remaining operation for this particular order).

The priority ratio therefore, for this order is:

$$\text{Priority Ratio} = \frac{42 \text{ days till needed}}{65 \text{ days work to be done}} = .65$$

The priority ratio of .65 represents the percentage of lead time left until the order is needed. In this case, 65 days of work remain to be done but the order will be needed in 42 days; it is behind schedule. The ratio of .65 means that 65% of the work remains to be done if the parts are to be ready on the required date of March 1.

In priority control, there are three conditions which can exist for any given order in relation to the schedule: On schedule, ahead of schedule, and behind schedule. Examples are:

$$\text{Priority Ratio} = \frac{5 \text{ days till needed}}{10 \text{ days work to be done}} = .5 = \text{Behind Schedule}$$

$$\text{Priority Ratio} = \frac{10 \text{ days till needed}}{10 \text{ days work to be done}} = 1.0 = \text{On Schedule}$$

$$\text{Priority Ratio} = \frac{20 \text{ days till needed}}{10 \text{ days work to be done}} = 2.0 = \text{Ahead of Schedule}$$

*Requirements are equal to the total of assemblies and service parts.

INTERNATIONAL MACHINERY, INC.
PARTS MANUFACTURING DIVISION
HOUSTON
PRIORITY CONTROL REPORT

LOT NUMBER	PART NUMBER	START DATE	LOT SIZE	CURRENT LOCATION	PRIORITY RATIO	COMMENTS
2162	PMD-77	8/21/80	2000	Dept. 12	0.13	
2935	PMD 432	8/19/80	300	14	1.25	Hold
2622	PMD 129	9/26/80	4500	10	0.00	Part Shortage
2450	PMD 365	8/30/80	10000	15	0.52	

Figure 11-1. Part Manufacturing Division: Priority Control Report.

Obviously, jobs behind schedule need to be expedited while jobs ahead of schedule should be delayed until the priority ratio is reduced to 1.0.

As a guideline, action to be taken on any given order depends on its priority ratio:

Priority Ratio	*Action To Be Taken*
0.00–0.99	Expedite. Run order with lowest ratio first.
1.00–9999	Delay manufacture until priority reaches 1.0 or below.

THE PRIORITY CONTROL REPORT

Figure 11-1 shows a section of Houston's priority control report used by production planning expediters and foremen to assign work and expedite orders behind schedule. As orders arrive in each department, foremen check the priority ratios for all orders and assign them to machines accordingly. In Figure 11-1, for example, the following priorities would have been established by foremen:

RUN PRIORITY	LOT NUMBER	PRIORITY RATIO
1st	2622	0.00—If part arrives on time.
2nd	2162	0.13
3rd	2450	0.52
4th	2935	1.25

Foremen, moreover, must take into account groupings of orders to minimize set-up time on machines. Set-up time can be minimized through careful scheduling, and foremen should be given some flexibility in modestly rearranging priorities.

The priority control system is flexible and can handle exceptions easily. When machines break down or when inventory changes are discovered by foremen and expeditors, orders can be reassigned on the spot to account for changes.

12

Production Planning and Control: Inventory Control Practices

"One of the greatest failings of today's executive is his inability to do what he's supposed to do."

Malcolm Kent

The fourth component of successful production planning and control is inventory control, and it all begins with an inventory plan which management develops to support return-on-asset goals (see Chapter 2).

THE INVENTORY PLAN

Figure 12-1 is an illustration of PMD's inventory plan projected during October, 1980 for the 1981 fiscal year. It is reported in dollars rather than increments of inventory, because inventory is an investment in dollars and it is reflected as such in the company's return-on-asset goals.

Part #1 of Figure 12-1 shows the dollar values of inventory, quarter by quarter, for 1981, while Part #2 of Figure 12-1 shows the actions to be generated to support the plan. In actual practice a detailed inventory plan by product line would be forecast in categories of purchased parts, manufactured parts, and finished goods to further define the inventory plan.

The inventory plan is an excellent tool for determining inventory objectives which are aimed at achieving the company's profit plan.

INTERNATIONAL MACHINERY, INC.
PARTS MANUFACTURING DIVISION
1981 INVENTORY PLAN
($000)

Plan Developed: 10/15/80

FORECASTED SHIPMENTS	1ST. QTR.	2ND. QTR.	3RD. QTR.	4TH. QTR.
Net shipments	$12,200	$10,500	$13,000	$ 9,000
Net shipments YTD	12,200	22,700	35,700	44,700
Cost of goods sold	7,000	6,000	7,400	5,100
Cost of goods sold YTD	7,000	13,000	20,400	25,500
INVENTORY PLAN				
Gross inventory	$ 4,220	$ 3,825	$ 4,555	$ 4,550
Less: Obsolescence	(20)	(5)	(5)	(0)
Less: Inventory disposal	(200)	(20)	(50)	(50)
Net inventory	$ 4,000	$ 3,800	$ 4,500	$ 4,500
Net inventory YTD	$ 4,000	$ 7,800	$12,300	$16,800
Inventory Turnover	1.75	1.67	1.66	1.52

Figure 12-1. Part 1. Parts Manufacturing Division: Inventory plan.

Remember that inventory constitutes one of the largest categories of return-on-assets calculations, and failure to adhere to the plan could prove ruinous. The inventory plan forces the development of actions to keep inventory levels in line with sales levels.

REDUCING EXCESS AND OBSOLETE INVENTORIES

In many companies inventory reduction follows a familiar pattern. Purchasing plans are curtailed, vendor shipments reduced or canceled, work forces are slashed, and transfers of the remaining people effected. All of these actions, of course, reduce inventories, and top management breathes a sigh of relief.

Soon, however, delivery problems erupt. Customer promise dates slip, lead times erode, quality problems increase, and gaps in the work flow create manufacturing inefficiencies. Management reacts by stepping-up purchasing commitments, rehiring laid-off workers, and pumping more inventory into manufacturing.

Lead times firm up, delivery promises improve, and manufacturing efficiencies are made. Inventories increase, and a new round of inventory reductions are ready to start again. The cycle is seemingly endless.

INTERNATIONAL MACHINERY, INC.
PARTS MANUFACTURING DIVISION
1981 INVENTORY PLAN

ASSUMPTIONS
Net Shipments of $44,700,000
Inventory Disposal of $320,000

INVENTORY INCREASES
Net inventory will increase $500,000 during 1981 to match shipment increases projected for
the same year. The increases will be in:

Plastics machinery parts	$400,000
Stainless steel couplings	$100,000

INVENTORY DECREASES
The recession and subsequent sales drop in the petrochemical field will cause the following
inventory decrease:

High pressure fittings	$150,000

Figure 12-1. Part 2. Parts Manufacturing Division: Inventory plan.

All of what has just been described happens because managements
too many times do the wrong things to reduce inventory. They cut safety
stocks (the easiest target), and move high turnover stocks even faster
than before; too fast, in fact. They are made to move faster than they
are replaced. Since safety stocks were established to provide for tardy
vendor deliveries, machine problems, and many other factors, their
reduction can, and does, lead to stock-cuts at critical times.

The decision to reduce inventories must take into account the utility
of the parts. Parts of low utility should be the focus of inventory reduction programs; they are classified as either obsolete or excess inventory.

Both classifications of inventory-excess and obsolete-result from
engineering changes, shifts in customer demand, cost reduction of parts,
quality problems, and planning errors. These factors will always be
present, so the manufacturing manager can always expect to face the
problem of reducing both excess and inventory levels.

The identification and reduction of excess and obsolete inventories
involves these steps:

1. Identification of both classifications of inventory by part number
   and quantities.
2. Periodic auditing of the inventory system to detect changes in
   excess and obsolete parts.

3. Cancellation and revision of purchasing and manufacturing orders to reduce the impact of unusable inventory.
4. Use of a company program to rework, sell, or otherwise dispose of the unusable inventory.
5. Recognition in the accounting procedure for excess and obsolete inventory reserves.

The latter point is particularly significant. Companies will tend to hold onto obsolete and excess inventory because scrapping of them leads to an inventory loss with its attendant negative effect on profits. The use of reserves to provide for disposal will assure those inventories don't expand. Their impact on both profitability and return-on-assets can be anticipated.

PMD has used the same inventory reduction program in all of its three plants. First, inventory control people periodically identify obsolete and excess inventories by part number and quantities. Computer reports are issued containing the information.

A competition to see who can reduce inventories the most ensues. *All* salaried people are encouraged to participate. Any participant can be assigned a group of part numbers to work with. It's on a first-come, first-served basis. Once assigned his or her group, those same part numbers are not available to anybody else. As expected, everybody goes after the larger dollar items. Engineers, foremen, production planners, and other salaried people then try to modify the parts so they can be used as other, active parts in the inventory; or they attempt any number of stratagems to either make the parts usable or find some company (such as the original vendor) who will buy them at reduced value for their inventory.

The program has been a success. Successful participants are recognized by management through published reports and on their performance reviews. Recognition appears to be the factor motivating most of the people in the program.

THE ABC INVENTORY SYSTEM

In any company which manufactures or assembles a great deal of parts, an analysis of part usage will reveal that a relatively small number of parts constitute the greater share of volume. In many cases 10 to 20% of the established part numbers account for 75 to 80% of production. These are called "A" parts.

"C" parts generally account for 50% of the issued part numbers but only 10% or less of production.

Those parts that are left are classified as "B" parts.

The relationship of the ABC inventory showing the number of part numbers and dollar value of those part numbers can be seen in Figure 12-2.

ABC analysis has many uses in inventory control. Some applications are:

1. Identification of "A" and "B" items in excess and obsolete inventory lists to direct attention to reduction of those inventories where it will do the most good.

2. Concentration of "A" and "B" items in the scheduling process, production plan, and priority control system since they represent the overwhelming share of inventory value.

3. Application of larger than normal safety stocks to "C" items to reduce stock-outs and improve customer service. Since "C" items are low cost inventory, a small increase in safety stock levels will be a worthwhile investment.

DETERMINATION OF LOT SIZES

Included in every calculation for parts requirements in an MRP program (or manual system) is a method for determination of optimum lot sizes in manufacturing. Lot sizes are important to manufacturing managers because the larger the lot sizes are the fewer the number of setups and the higher the level of operator performance will be.

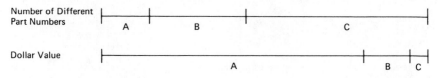

Figure 12-2. ABC inventory graph: Comparison of the number of different part numbers to their dollar value.

There is, however, a catch! As lot sizes increase so does the level of inventory investment increase, and the attainment of delivery promises for shipping products to customers decreases.

The relationship of lot sizes to inventory levels is pictured in Figure 12-3. Notice that the average inventory level is equal to one-half the lot size plus the safety stock. Visualize an increase in lot sizes and observe the correspondant increase in the average inventory level. Conversely, visualize a drop in the lot size and it is plain to see the decrease in average inventory.

From this relationship, a general rule of inventory can be gleaned: *In manufacturing, lot size is the major determinant of inventory levels, and any increase or decrease in lot sizes will have a major impact on inventory investment.* It is, therefore, very important to regulate lot sizes in manufacturing to balance the relationship of lot size to inventory.

ECONOMIC ORDER QUANTITIES

Set-up and ordering costs are realized whenever a plant changes set-ups on machines or purchases parts and materials. As just mentioned, these costs can be alleviated by increasing lot sizes in both manufacturing and purchasing. As a general rule, high inventory ("A") parts which have low set-up and ordering costs should have small lot sizes. On the other

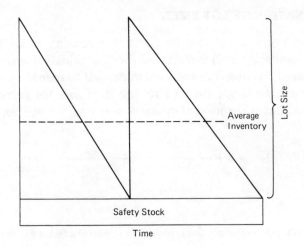

Figure 12-3. The relationship of lot sizes to average inventory.

hand, "B" and "C" parts with high set-up and ordering costs should have large lot sizes.

The relationship just described has been expressed mathematically in a formula referred to as the "Economic Order Quantity (EOQ)." The EOQ balances set-up and ordering costs vs. lot sizes and determines optimum lot sizes based on economics. The formula is:

$$EOQ = \sqrt{\frac{2(\text{Annual Usage} \times (\text{Set-Up} + \text{Order Cost})}{\text{Cost Per Part} \times \text{Carrying Cost}}}$$

Let's determine the EOQ for PMD-216, a ½" pin produced at Los Angeles. To do this, certain information must first be known, as seen here:

Part No. and Name	PMD-216, 1/2" Pin
Annual usage	10,000
Cost per unit	$ 0.50
Order cost	$10.00
Set-up cost	$40.00
Carrying cost	$ 0.30[1]

Calculation of the EOQ follows:

$$EOQ = \sqrt{\frac{2\,(10{,}000) \times (\$10 + \$40)}{.50 \times .30}}$$

$$EOQ = \sqrt{\frac{1{,}000{,}000}{.15}}$$

$$EOQ = 2582 \text{ Pieces}$$

Balancing all costs, it would be *theoretically* best to purchase PMD-216 in quantities of 2582 or, if manufactured in the plant, to plan lot sizes of 2582 pieces.

The word "theoretically" was stressed because the EOQ represents static numbers. In reality, the factors which determine EOQ's change frequently. Annual usage, for example, will fluctuate year to year; car-

[1]Carrying cost = costs to carry the part: Insurance, taxes, storage, obsolescence and handling.

rying costs will change due to price increases and cost reduction efforts; other costs will have the same pressures.

It is best to regenerate EOQ's annually (there should be a computer program to handle this task efficiently). It is also best to apply EOQ's to "A" and some "B" items, while lot sizes for the remaining "B" and all of the "C" items can be based on historical data; their impact on EOQ economics should be minimal, simply because their value is low. Attempting to apply EOQ's to *all* parts may be too mammoth a task if the plant carries thousands of parts on its active part number roster.

13
Control of Purchasing

"The buyer needs a hundred eyes, the seller not one."

Proverb

In most manufacturing companies, purchasing of parts and materials constitutes a large share of manufacturing costs. This can range from 20 to 80% of cost-of-goods-sold, and probably averages 40 to 50% for most companies.

PMD, during 1981 purchased parts valued at $10 million; this was 40% of their $25 million cost-of-goods-sold. It is clear that control of this activity is vital to the success of any manufacturing enterprise. Escalating purchase prices make control of purchasing even more of a mandate.

THE PURCHASING BUDGET

The first elements of control in purchasing are unit and dollar planning. Planning the purchasing budget allows purchasing managers to think through objectives clearly and plan for cost reductions. The purchasing budget is generally made in two parts—units and dollars. In actual practice, each purchasing agent plans his own product line purchases for the forthcoming fiscal year.

Figure 13-1 is an example of how Los Angeles' purchasing agents plan their purchases. Using part #PMD-12 as an example, the purchasing agent is informed of production requirements for the year, and then with knowledge of inventory levels, plans to purchase those quantities needed to support the production schedule. He performs these calculations—as shown in Figure 13-1—for all of the parts and materials he will need to purchase in the new fiscal year.

After unit purchasing budgets have been made and approved, the purchasing budget in dollars is prepared. Standard costs for different part numbers are calculated and then fed into the computer files. These costs then become the standard purchasing costs for the year.

The final purchasing budget in dollars is summarized in a report illustrated in Figure 13-2. Again, requirements and current inventories are used to project purchasing dollars to be spent in the new year. The format of the report is similar to the one used for the unit purchasing budget.

PURCHASING PRICE VARIANCES

Once that standard costs have been established, some form of control is needed to assure the budget is being maintained. Control in purchasing is practiced by comparing standard costs vs. actual costs by individual purchasing agent. Should each purchasing agent be so fortunate as to keep his product line purchases under standard cost, then a favorable variance will result. If, on the other hand, prices rise above standard cost, then a negative variance will result. A resourceful purchasing agent should have little trouble, in most cases, in maintaining standard costs. Quantity discounts, freight allowances, favorable contracts with new vendors, and other tactics are employed by most purchasing agents to assure favorable variances.

INTERNATIONAL MACHINERY, INC.
PARTS MANUFACTURING DIVISION
UNIT PURCHASING BUDGET
(000)

PMD—12	TOTAL	1ST. QTR.	2ND. QTR.	3RD. QTR.	4TH. QTR.
Requirements	450	85	160	160	45
Less: Beginning inventory	25	25	55	55	20
Sub-total	425	60	105	105	25
Plus: Ending inventory	25	55	55	20	25
Purchasing quantity	450	115	160	125	50

Figure 13-1. Parts Manufacturing Division: unit purchasing budget.

INTERNATIONAL MACHINERY, INC.
PARTS MANUFACTURING DIVISION
DOLLAR PURCHASING BUDGET
($000)

	TOTAL	QTR.	QTR.	QTR.	QTR.
Cost of materials	$2100	$ 510	$ 600	$ 540	$ 450
Less: Beginning inventory	170	170	210	170	160
Sub-total	$1930	$ 340	$ 390	$ 370	$ 290
Plus: Ending inventory	170	210	170	160	170
Purchasing dollars	$2100	$ 550	$ 560	$ 530	$ 460

Figure 13-2. Parts Manufacturing Division: dollar purchasing budget.

Price variances in purchasing follow a generally predictable curve. As seen in Figure 13-3 favorable variances to standard are usually obtained during the first half of the year while unfavorable variances are generated during the latter half of the year. This occurs because purchasing agents try to protect their price levels by contracts, and those contracts generally extend into the start of the new fiscal year. As soon as the contracts expire, sellers escalate prices, and the new goods are purchased at prices above forecasted standard costs.

Favorable price variances, then, should be obtained during the first half of the fiscal year, and should be large enough to offset unfavorable

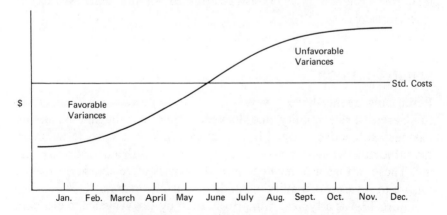

Figure 13-3. The price variance curve in purchasing.

variances of the last half of the year plus whatever reductions to standard cost have been pledged in a cost reduction program.

For the past fiscal year, Los Angeles' purchasing manager had anticipated a budget of $2 million (standard cost) and his buyers projected cost savings of $100,000 (favorable variance). If everything went according to plan, the purchasing budget would have been $2 million for the entire year. Let's see how they did:

MONTH	STANDARD COST		VARIANCES	
	SCHEDULED PURCHASES	ACTUAL PURCHASES	MONTH	YTD
Jan.	$225,000	$200,000	−25,000	− 25,000
Feb.	187,000	167,000	−20,000	− 45,000
Mar.	169,000	150,000	−19,000	− 64,000
Apr.	190,000	160,000	−30,000	− 94,000
May	170,000	150,000	−20,000	−114,000
Jun.	160,000	140,000	−20,000	−134,000
Jul.	150,000	155,000	+ 5,000	−129,000
Aug.	140,000	150,000	+10,000	−119,000
Sept.	180,000	185,000	+ 5,000	−114,000
Oct.	130,000	140,000	+10,000	−104,000
Nov.	140,000	145,000	+ 5,000	− 99,000
Dec.	159,000	163,000	+ 4,000	− 95,000
	$2,000,000	$1,905,000		

Since the goal was $2 million for the year, and since actual purchases at standard cost were $1,905,000 the goal was missed by $5,000 but a favorable variance of $95,000 was attained for the year. Not a bad performance!

VENDOR RATINGS

Purchasing agents have always rated the performance of vendors in three areas: Price, quality, and delivery. While most of that evaluation has been subjective, a trend has developed in recent years to augment the subjective evaluation of vendor performance with a quantitative rating. These ratings are meant to provide a basis of vendor performance for use in reviewing, qualifying, and comparing vendors.

Figure 13-4 is a typical rating form used by Los Angeles to evaluate

INTERNATIONAL MACHINERY, INC.
PARTS MANUFACTURING DIVISION
LOS ANGELES PLANT
VENDOR RATING REPORT

Part Name: 1″ Liner Part Number: PMD—32

	VENDOR #1	VENDOR #2	VENDOR #3
PRICE			
A. Unit Price	$1.00	$1.10	$1.20
B. $\dfrac{\text{Lowest Price}}{\text{Net Price}} \times 100$	100	91	83
C. Price Rating (Line C × .40)	40.0	36.4	33.2
QUALITY			
A. Lots received	80	80	60
B. Lots accepted	72	77	53
C. Percent accepted	90.0	96.3	88.3
D. Quality rating (Line C × .35)	31.5	33.7	30.9
DELIVERY			
A. Delivery promises kept	95%	93%	100%
B. Delivery rating (Line B × .25)	23.8	23.3	25.0
TOTAL RATING			
Add: Price—Line C	40.0	36.4	33.2
Quality—Line D	31.5	33.7	30.9
Delivery—Line B	23.8	23.3	24.0
Total Rating	95.3	93.4	89.1

Note: This table is an adaptation of a weighted-point vendor rating plan of the National Association of Purchasing Agents.

Figure 13-4. Parts Manufacturing Division: Los Angeles Plant: Vendor rating report.

vendor performance. It compares the performance of three vendors (in this case) in the areas of price, quality, and delivery of part number, PMD-32, a 1″ liner. An explanation of the use of the form follows:

Price

A. Unit Price. This is the gross price less quantity discounts; transportation charges are included.

B. $\dfrac{\text{Lowest Price}}{\text{Net Price}} \times 100$ — the calculation yields a reference point for any vendor's price compared with the lowest price submitted. For, example, vendor #2 is charging $0.10 more per unit, and yielding, in the calculation, a rating of 91 percent.

C. Price Rating—As you will see momentarily, a perfect rating for any vendor is 100% based on perfection in all three categories of performance:

Price	40%
Quality	35%
Delivery	25%
Total	100%

This is referred to as a weighted plan, with price being weighted the heaviest, delivery the least, and quality in-between.

The price rating is obtained by multiplying the weight factor (.40) by the result obtained in line "B".

Quality

A. Lots Received. This refers to the number of lots received from the vendor during the given period of time (normally one year).

B. Lots Accepted. The number of lots accepted by receiving inspection is written here.

C. Percent Accepted. The percentage of lots accepted is calculated:

$$\% \text{ Lots Accepted} = \frac{\text{number of lots accepted}}{\text{number of lots received}} \times 100$$

D. Quality Rating. Line "C" is multiplied by .35 to obtain the quality rating.

Delivery

A. Delivery promises kept—if a vendor submits 100 lots during the year and 90 are accepted, the delivery promises kept would be 90%.

B. Delivery Rating. Multiply line "A" by .25.

Total Rating

The price, quality, and delivery ratings are added together for each vendor to obtain the final rating.

Vendor ratings are an effective measure of control over vendor performance. They signify to the purchasing manager who is doing the job, and who is falling down. Those vendors found to be deficient in any one or more of the three key areas then have the opportunity to correct his performance.

14
Control of Manufacturing Quality

"Do it right or don't do it at all!"

Popular Quality Control Saying

Quality today is the last frontier for profit improvement and cost reduction, and nowhere is this more so than in manufacturing.

Improvements in manufacturing have focused on manpower reductions, tooling and methods improvements, incentive systems, MRP programs, and a host of other approaches and programs designed to reduce costs and improve manufacturing profitability. But relatively little has been accomplished in the area of quality to achieve the same goals. While some progress has been made, the full potential of quality as a contributing factor to manufacturing success has not been realized. Effective quality techniques and controls can contribute to both improved profitability and repeat sales (through enhanced customer satisfaction.)

To be successful, the quality program in manufacturing needs to encompass the following elements:

A. A cost-of-quality reporting system which indicates the success (or failure) of the quality program.
B. A thorough and ongoing and detailed evaluation of the quality system.

C. A quality plan which lists all improvements needed to upgrade quality, including objectives, responsible parties, and timetables.

D. A company (or divisional) quality board to establish manufacturing quality policy and which concerns itself with major quality problems and opportunities.

E. A successful vendor quality program.

F. An effective production quality program.

G. A responsive quality audit of outgoing products to customers (responsive in the sense that it is timely and evokes immediate corrective action of problems found).

Let's examine each of these factors in some detail:

COST-OF-QUALITY

Cost-of-quality means exactly what it says—a detailing of all quality costs. Unfortunately in many manufacturing organizations many of the elements of the true cost picture are omitted. Some companies claim only scrap and rework costs while others include cost of inspectors, and so on. To be properly inclusive an effective cost-of-quality report should include the following elements:

1. *Warranty Costs* are those costs which reflect failure of the product to perform its intended function (or those which displease the customer esthetically). Included are those costs attributable to customer complaint investigations and of returned goods inspection, sorting, and testing.

2. *Scrap Costs* are incurred when parts and materials are deemed to become totally worthless (disregarding scrap value) because of quality problems. Scrap costs should always include material, labor, and overhead apportioned to the product.

3. *Rework Costs* also include material, labor, and overhead which results when defective product is sorted, inspected, tested, and reworked to recover the parts or materials for usable inventory. This does *not* include costs billable to vendors for their quality errors.

4. *Appraisal Costs* are those costs associated with inspecting the product to assume compliance with company specifications for purchased parts and materials, manufactured parts, and finished product. Also included are costs to inspect the manufacturing process and costs

to determine vendor quality capability. Since both of these latter costs directly influence the quality of products they are considered part of appraisal costs.

5. *Administration Costs* are essentially quality control budgetary costs less inspection labor. Typical administrative costs are salaries for quality control managers, foremen, technicians, and engineers, and support costs such as testing costs, gauging costs, calibration costs, and other miscellaneous costs reflected in the quality control budget.

6. *Engineering Costs* are those costs incurred in both marketing and engineering to improve product quality. Typical engineering costs are:

Design Reviews: These are costs incurred in the review of new products or major design changes of existing products to improve quality and eliminate quality problems prior to the relase of product drawings.

Product qualification: This refers to costs incurred in the testing, pilot plant, and qualification of new products or for major changes in existing product lines.

Design changes: These costs occur when design changes are necessary to correct original design inadequacies.

PMD's divisional level cost-of-quality (COQ) report is shown in Figure 14-1. Section "A," "COQ Summary" shows COQ as a percent of sales. Since COQ numbers, by themselves, are absolute numbers they are meaningless until related to some base figure such as sales. This is because a company with $100,000 quality costs and a sales base of $1 million has a COQ of 10%, while another company with $50,000 quality costs and a sales base of $250,000 has a 20% COQ.

The divisional COQ summary publishes statistics for the current month, YTD, and last year's average. The chart also illustrates monthly COQ readings and the COQ trend. Notice that the trend shown in Figure 14-1 is down.

The next section, "COQ Categories" lists costs for all COQ categories and indicates what their percent of sales are for the current month and YTD. This refinement of COQ dollars shows where the "COQ dollars are." It helps managers to focus on meaningful categories for quality cost reduction.

The last section of the report "Highlights" indicates the major actions, improvements, and problems of the month. It is a good tool for quality control people to get their message across and get management's attention.

**INTERNATIONAL MACHINERY, INC.
PARTS MANUFACTURING DIVISION
COST-OF-QUALITY
DIVISION LEVEL PERFORMANCE**

A. COQ SUMMARY

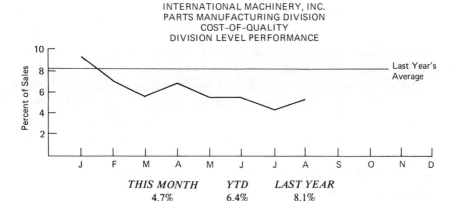

	THIS MONTH	YTD	LAST YEAR
	4.7%	6.4%	8.1%

B. MAJOR COQ CATEGORIES

COQ CATEGORY	DOLLARS		PERCENT	
	THIS MONTH	YTD	THIS MONTH	YTD
Warranty	$ 3,200	$ 45,600	.4	.4
Scrap	8,800	88,500	1.1	1.8
Rework	7,200	57,300	.9	1.3
Appraisal (Inspection)	14,400	160,950	1.8	2.1
Administration	3,120	26,910	.4	.6
Engineering Support	805	14,025	.1	.2
Total COQ	$37,525	$393,285	4.7	6.4

C. HIGHLIGHTS

1. The NC tools at Houston and Pittsburgh are now fully on-stream and producing at normal yields which has reduced scrap and rework.
2. Warranty costs will decrease when the field upgrade program for plastics machinery parts is completed in about three months.

Figure 14-1. Parts Manufacturing Division: Cost-of-quality.

In actual practice, each plant in the PMD system has its own COQ report. The divisional level summary discussed here is a compilation of COQ statistics of the three plants.

QUALITY SYSTEM EVALUATION

Cost-of-quality is a reflection of how effectively the quality function is being utilized. It does not, however, guide the organization to perform the right tasks to accomplish the quality mission. That is the job of the quality system evaluation.

The quality system evaluation is a questionnaire aimed at assuring that the company is doing the right things to achieve high quality products at low quality costs. It encompasses a rating technique to enable manufacturing management to assess the degree of development of the quality control function in each plant. The rating system consists of four degrees of development for each of the functions and activities being evaluated. These are:

Rating	Points Awarded	Explanation of Rating
Outstanding	5	Activities and functions awarded this rating have highly effective and sophisticated development.
Good	3	This rating is given to activities and functions producing acceptable results.
Adequate	1	Activities and functions rated adequate are those where there is minimum development but much remains to be done to become effective.
Poor	0	A poor rating is given when either no work or little work has been done to develop the activity or function.

Let's now look at PMD's quality system evaluation format.

INTERNATION MACHINERY, INC.
PARTS MANUFACTURING DIVISION
QUALITY SYSTEM EVALUATION

Plant _____Evaluation Date _____

Total Rating _____

Policy, Objectives, Administration	5	3	1	0
1. Is there a quality policy, and does it cover all applicable areas of operation? Is it clear and understandable? Is it practical?				
2. Does QC have realistic objectives to accomplish annually, and are they assigned to the right people to assure they can be accomplished? Are specific duties and time tables established?				
3. Is there a quality manual which explains all major practices and procedures for QC? Is it updated and current? Do the right people have copies? Is the manual used and followed?				
4. Is QC a respected function in the company? Is it involved with all departments? Does it receive cooperation from other departments?				
5. Does QC have adequate facilities and budget to accomplish its mission? Are they being utilized properly?				

	5	3	1	0

Organization

1. Is the caliber of the people in QC adequate to handle the job? Are they technically proficient? Do they understand that quality is a profit contributor as will as a technical specialty?

2. Are manning levels adequate? Are they excessive? Are there too many inspectors and not enough quality engineers?

3. Is AQ geared to handle quality improvement as well as the day-to-day activities?

4. Are QC members trained well? Do they know exactly what their jobs are and what they need to accomplish? Are they engaged in studies to improve their performance?

Quality Costs and Reports

1. Is there a COQ program? Is it clear and understandable? Does it generate corrective action? Is it used by manufacturing supervisors?

2. Are quality performance reports (showing lots defective) clear and usable? Do manufacturing supervisors understand them and use them? Do they generate action? Do they contain the right information?

3. Are quality records (both performance and COQ) maintained in a

5	3	1	0

safe, restricted area? Are records retained for sufficient periods to meet federal and state laws? Are those records accessible and easy to find when specific records are needed for legal reasons?

Manufacturing Quality Planning

1. Are critical and major quality characteristics identified on engineering drawings? Are they understandable to inspectors, operators, and foremen? Are potential quality problems high-lighted through proper inspection instructions?

2. Does QC participate in design reviews for new products and for major changes to existing products? Does manufacturing review the adequacy of tooling, gauging, and testing equipment?

3. Are new products given a test run in manufacturing before production begins? Are field evaluations made of the new products to test customer reaction? Does quality engineering use the test run to plan and refine inspection test methods and procedures?

4. Are machine and process capability studies made for new equipment and tooling? Are operators and inspectors trained in the proper use of new equipment? Are their instructions adequate?

5	3	1	0

5. Are effective sampling plans developed for new products and processes? Are inspectors trained in their use? Are salvage procedures developed to prevent the mixing of acceptable and rejected product?

Vendor Control
1. Are vendors qualified to produce an acceptable product before they are awarded a contract? Is a quality rating plan used to evaluate vendor quality capability along with price and delivery?

2. Are quality requirements clearly communicated to vendors? Do they receive all updated engineering drawings?

3. Are vendors promptly notified of quality problems? Are they responsive to getting the problems corrected? Does QC monitor poor quality vendors? Are changes made quickly enough to prevent quality from deteriorating further?

Receiving Inspection
1. Do receiving inspectors have clear and comprehensive instructions and sampling plans? Are identification and classification of quality characteristics the same between vendors and receiving inspectors?

2. Are rejection and salvage precedors workable? Is defective material sep-

5	3	1	0

arated from acceptable material? Are samples of defective material given to vendors?

3. Is a quality rating system used to document vendor performance? Are there complete lot acceptance and rejection history files for all vendors?

Manufacturing Quality Control
1. Do operators sample their own work? Is time for quality included in the work standard? Are foremen actively involved in corrective action?

2. Is the type of inspection adequate? Is it containing the defects within the department rather than finding them in subsequent operations? When defects are found, are they being properly traced to the operations that caused them?

3. Are gages—used by operators and inspectors—calibrated? Are calibration procedures adequate to prevent wrong acceptance or rejection because of improper gage calibration? Are records maintained for each major gage showing calibration dates and repair history?

4. Are engineering drawings used by production and quality employees up to-date? Are drawings changed when revisions are made or are revisions "penciled-in" by product engineers?

5	3	1	0

5. Does manufacturing participate in decisions affecting rejected parts? Are the right part disposition decisions being made? Do performance reports realistically reflect the level of quality in each area?

Finished Product Audit
1. Are quality audits made of products that have been accepted by QC and are ready for shipment? Are the results of those audits fed back to departments responsible for defects found in the audit? Is corrective action effective?

2. Are defects found during the product audit correlated with defects found in manufacturing to detect trends and take positive corrective action?

Shipping, Warehousing, and Packing
1. Are products packaged to prevent damage in-transit? Are handling procedures designed to minimize damage? Are damage problems reported and analyzed? Is someone assigned in the company to act as "Packaging Engineer" to resolve these problems?

2. Are goods stored in such a way as to prevent damage and spoilage? Are goods rotated? Is there a first-in first-out system of warehousing?

Customer Satisfaction
1. Are warranty problems fully investigated? Are representative failed

5	3	1	0

parts analyzed? Are returned goods analyzed? Is there a test lab for failure analysis?

2. Are files on product failures found by customers analyzed to detect trends? Are those trends correlated with manufacturing quality problems? Are field quality problems told to supervisors?

3. Are periodic surveys made of customer satisfaction? Are those surveys used to spot problems and take corrective action?

4. Does the customer receive adequate service once the warranty has expired? Are servicemen trained to handle customer problems? Are they trained to identify quality problems and to relate them to the factory?

The quality system evaluation has the following minimum and maximum point potentials:

CATEGORY	NO. OF PARTS	MINIMUM POINTS	MAXIMUM POINTS
Policy, objectives, administration	5	0	25
Organization	4	0	20
Quality costs and reports	3	0	15
Manufacturing quality planning	5	0	25
Vendor control	3	0	15
Receiving inspection	3	0	15
Manufacturing quality control	5	0	25
Finished product audit	2	0	10
Shipping, warehousing, packing	2	0	10
Customer satisfaction	4	0	20
	36	0	180

A perfect quality system could achieve 180 points (practically impossible to do) while no quality system at all would receive no points (also approaching the impossible—even the smallest manufacturing concern will need some quality systems).

A fully evaluated quality system would need the following points to achieve the rating indicated below:

RATING	POINTS AWARDED PER PART	TOTAL POINTS
Outstanding	5	160–180
Good	3	108–159
Adequate	1	56–107
Poor		0–55

THE QUALITY PLAN

To be really successful, a company just completing its quality system evaluation must identify its weaknesses and establish a plan to overcome them. This is referred to as the quality plan. Figure 14-2 is a page from the quality plan developed by PMD's Pittsburgh plant.

Problems are identified, actions are specified, persons responsible for the actions are identified, and dates for completion of the actions are indicated.

The quality plan should *always* have the blessing and support of top management if anything is to get done. This point is particularly relevant when it is recognized that manufacturing people alone cannot make all the needed improvements; engineering and marketing people are also involved.

THE QUALITY BOARD

Any ongoing quality program needs direction. It is simply not enough to turn full responsibility for quality improvement over to the quality control manager; too many other people are involved. The quality control manager cannot design, manufacture, or sell and service the product. These jobs rightfully belong to engineering, manufacturing, and marketing. These are the people who have the primary influence upon

INTERNATIONAL MACHINERY, INC.
PARTS MANUFACTURING DIVISION
PITTSBURGH
QUALITY PLAN

PROBLEM	ACTION TO BE TAKEN	PERSONS RESPONSIBLE	DATE FOR COMPLETION
No identification of quality costs.	Develop a COQ report	QC Manager	3/81
Inspectors are confused about relative seriousness of quality characteristics.	Identify critical quality characteristics on engineering drawings.	QC Supervisor and Engineering Manager	1/82
Excessive defective parts are escaping the machine shop.	Improve sampling plans used by inspectors.	Quality Engineer	6/81
There is no early warning of quality problems found by customers.	Start a finished goods audit.	QC Auditor	2/81

Figure 14-2. Parts Manufacturing Division: Qualtiy plan.

quality and, consequently, they affect quality results the most. They must become involved.

Each company or division of a company needs a quality board to direct the quality efforts of its people. The quality board should become involved with quality in the following areas:

Quality Policy
Quality Improvement
Major Quality Problems

The quality board, then, assumes the mantle of responsibility for the quality success of the company. Their job is to monitor major actions and results to assure the right things are done by the right people at the right time. It assures direct involvement in quality of every operating and support arm of the company.

The quality is very important to the manufacturing manager. There is a tendency in any manufacturing company to lay the total blame for poor quality on the doorstep of manufacturing. In almost every case that is not true. Sloppy design practices, misunderstandings between marketing people and customers regarding product needs, poor service—these and a host of other factors are directly attributable to engineering and marketing. The quality board provides an opportunity to objectively analyze quality problems and assign responsibility for corrective action to the right parties.

The quality board should generally have this composition:

> General Manager—Chairman
> Quality Control Manager—Secretary
> Manufacturing Manager
> Engineering Manager
> Marketing Manager

It is essential that the general manager assume responsibility for quality results by chairing the quality board. His leadership will also preclude the dominance of vested interests above actions best for the company.

VENDOR QUALITY

Chapter 13 described a vendor rating system for evaluating the price, quality, and delivery capability of vendors. In it, vendor quality ratings were determined by lot acceptance criteria:

$$\% \text{ Lot Acceptance} = \frac{\text{No. of Lots Accepted}}{\text{No. of Lots Inspected}} \times 100$$

In my experience this measurement is the simplest and best to use for evaualion of vendor quality. Other complex ratings have been developed by quality practitioners but they tend to become so hard to understand that they lose their meaning. The use of acceptance rates, shown above, tells it all about vendor performance.

The control of vendor quality also demands some other activities:

1. Use of vendor history files to list lot acceptance rates by part numbers on dates received, rejections made, visits to and by vendors and listing of problems discussed, actions taken by vendors to correct quality problems and a summary of their effectiveness.

2. Insistence by *purchasing* people that vendors correct quality prob-

lems, that timetables be established for corrective action, and that vendors will be eliminated as a source of supply if quality doesn't improve.

3. Evaluation of new suppliers' quality capability and their full understanding of the company's quality requirements.

4. Fast correction of rejected quality parts by vendors through rework or shipment of replacement parts.

THE PRODUCTION QUALITY PROGRAM

There are just a few basic ways that parts and materials can be inspected in manufacturing. These are:

First Piece Inspection

When the quality of the production run is dependent on the machine set-up, a first piece inspection needs to be made. Almost any operation utilizing tools, dies, jigs, and fixtures needs a first piece inspection. This type of inspection is usually best performed by a combination of set-up men *and* machine operators, the operators rechecking and verifying the adequacy of the set-up made by set-up men. Inspections are best left out of this sequence unless the first piece inspection demands specialized testing equipment. Once production people come to depend upon inspectors to check set-ups, they will not pay as close attention to the job. If they are held responsible for set-ups, they will do a better job and higher quality will result.

Roving Inspections

Here, inspectors move from machine to machine during the production run, checking parts. When production is generating either very high quality or very low quality parts this type of inspection is very effective. If quality is high there is no sense in using other more costly methods of inspection. Roving inspection is generally the least expensive method of inspection; a few inspectors can cover a lot of territory.

If quality levels are very poor, roving inspection will quickly detect failures, and inspectors will then be able to quarantine defective lots. The high rejection rate assures that defects will be found.

Tollgate Inspection

For most manufacturing operations, quality is neither very high nor very low; it falls somewhere in the middle. In this case inspectors, using the roving inspection method, are less likely to detect poor quality parts. When this is the case, tollgate inspection is called for.

In tollgate inspection, all completed lots of parts are funneled through a stationary inspection point at the end of each department. The product flow shown below illustrates tollgate inspection:

```
        Grinding Department—Grind Pins
                            Tollgate
        Milling Department  —Mill Slots in Pins
                            Tollgate
        Polishing Department—Polish Pins
                            Tollgate
                            Deliver To Assembly Dept.
```

Tollgate inspection is obviously most applicable to operations grouped together. For example, if all grinding machines are in one department a tollgate inspection can follow grinding. If many different types of operations are contained in one production department, tollgate inspection will probably be placed after key operations. To have it follow each and every operation would be too costly. For example:

```
Small Parts Department—Automatic Chucker—Thread Fitting
                        Chamfer Machine—Chamfer Fitting
                        Tapping Machine—Tap
                        Tollgate
                        Deliver To Assembly Department
```

Automatic Inspection. In this type of inspection, equipment inspects parts. This method of inspection is the fastest and most reliable, but also the costliest. It is generally applied to high cost, tight-tolerance parts where assembly operations are highly dependent on good parts.

Operator Inspection. It is *always* best to have operators check their own parts whenever possible, using an established sampling plan. This is probably one of the best inspection methods. It assures the interest of operators in quality, and reduces the number of inspectors needed in manufacturing. Operator inspection is generally used in partnership with either roving or tollgate inspection.

FINISHED GOODS AUDIT

It is always surprising to many people that once a product has been fully manufactured and ready for shipment to customers it contains defects. Invariably this is true. The real task of quality effectiveness, however, is the quantity of defects found in outgoing products and their degree of seriousness.

The finished goods audit is a final inspection of the product the way the customer sees it when he gets to use it. It's always conducted on product ready for shipment, and it is a reflection of (1) the quality level of products reaching customers, (2) the effectiveness of manufacturing in building a high-quality product, and (3) the effectiveness of the quality organization in releasing only high quality products for customers.

The finished goods audit is composed of quality characteristics important to customers and, hopefully, those same quality characteristics which are inspected in manufacturing.

The finished goods audit allows manufacturing management the opportunity to preview quality problems customers will find, and gives manufacturing people the opportunity to correct those problems before the finished goods warehouse is flooded with defective products.

15
Product Liability Defenses in Manufacturing

"The life of the law has not been logic; it has been experience."
Oliver Wendell Holmes, Jr.

During 1978 American manufacturers and retailers paid about $2.75 billion for product liability insurance. In 1976 almost 90,000 product liability lawsuits were filed. One expert in the field claims that the sum total of dollars in product liability is approaching 6% of the gross national product.

Staggering, isn't it? None of this was true, just a few short years ago. Plaintiffs in product liability law suits were charged with the burden of proof. This is no longer true. The doctrine of strict liability has changed that.

Strict liability is a doctrine that entitles the injured party to his day in court. In most cases the plantiff has only to prove that a defect in the product caused his or her injury. The plaintiff no longer has to prove negligence or carelessness on the part of the manufacturer. Awards of $1 million or more are no longer uncommon.

While much has been written recently about product liability little has been devoted to the manufacturing manager's role in product liability and those steps he must take to establish an ongoing product liability program and legal defense. That is my purpose here.

DESIGN CONSIDERATIONS

Although the responsibility for design rests with product engineering, manufacturing makes the design a reality. When manufacturing needs changes to design to attain manufacturing improvements or cost reduction, it cannot change either the design or the parts unilaterally. To assure integrity of design—a key element of successful claims defense—approval must first come from product engineering.

RECEIVING INSPECTION AND STOCK CONTROL

The purchase of parts must be guided by specifications established by engineering. Drawings and specifications must be clearly communicated to vendors. Vendors should be qualified as capable of delivering a quality product. Receiving inspection must assure that vendors are complying with established design criteria. Records must be maintained which show:

> Part number and name
> Vendor
> Date of purchase
> Date of vendor's manufacture
> Product identification numbers*
> *(lot numbers mostly)

Stock control is an essential part of an effective product liability program. Parts need to be properly identified and records of parts stocked and removed must be verified for accuracy. Inventory control practices should be aimed at eliminating shortages which require substitutions to be made on short notice.

MANUFACTURING PRACTICES

One of the most important aspects of a product liability program is the adequacy of training and written procedures covering the tasks performed in making the product. Clear instructions regarding operation of machinery in the plant, salvage procedures, inspection instructions, maintenance instructions, and job descriptions are those type of documents needed for proper claims defense in product liability. In a court of law, judges will weigh heavily the factor of such evidence on the grounds that a clear understanding of how to do the job is paramount to proper execution.

Manufacturing managers must create a distinction between critical parts and all other parts of the product. A critical part can be defined as that part which could cause a failure of the product resulting in injury to the user or damage to the environment. Normally, this is a job for engineering, but procedures used in manufacturing impact greatly. Therefore, it is to the advantage of the manufacturing manager to understand the role he plays in the handling of critical parts. Following are some of the major practices:

A. First, critical parts need to be defined. Manufacturing, marketing, engineering, and legal counsel should make those decisions.

B. There must be a receiving inspection function that stringently inspects those incoming critical parts.

C. Critical parts must be stored separately or with adequate controls to assure they are not "contaminated" by other goods. They, in other words, should not be exposed to other parts so mixes can occur.

D. Critical parts must be strictly controlled during the manufacturing process. The control of those parts will include proper inspection techniques, prevention of mixes, and identification of critical parts in manufacturing.

E. Records for critical parts must be maintained throughout the manufacturing process from receiving to shipping. Pertinent information will include vendor test results and a record of pieces accepted and rejected throughout each step of the manufacturing process.

F. All rejected critical parts need to be carefully segregated and accounted for throughout manufacturing. Records should be maintained which reflect corrective action (scrap, rework, etc.) and disposition of the parts.

G. All critical parts need to be fully inspected and tested throughout manufacturing and, most importantly, before shipment to customers.

H. Critical parts need to be properly marked and containerized prior to shipping.

I. In assembly operations, critical parts should arrive and be stored in segregated areas to prevent mixes.

J. Adequate records should be maintained and carefully monitored by quality control to assure that these parts cannot be passed from one operation to another without having first been inspected.

K. Critical parts should be clearly marked to prevent mixes in assembly. This factor is particularly important when differences between critical parts and other parts are small, and the possibility of using the wrong parts is high.

L. Careful decisions should be made about critical part sampling procedures. Some very sensitive parts (parts highly probable to cause failure if not manufactured properly) will probably need 100% individual inspection. Others, of a less sensitive nature, may be controlled through random lot sampling, using a reliable statistical sampling plan.

Probably, the best advice that can be given to manufacturing people regarding product liability is *not to try to do it yourself!* Get both competent legal counsel and hire an expert in the field of product liability to establish your program.

16
Control of Maintenance

"The unfortunate thing about this world is that good habits are so much easier to give up than bad ones."

Somerset Maugham

The control of maintenance operations is essential to good plant performance. Reports designed to disclose all important aspects of maintenance are needed by manufacturing managers to stay on top of maintenance costs and performance. These reports are:

1. Labor performance
2. Schedules missed
3. Craftsman performance
4. Machine maintenance costs

Each of these control documents are examined in the following pages.

LABOR PERFORMANCE

Labor performance in maintenance operations is one of the most difficult of all manufacturing jobs to achieve. The work is highly nonrepetitive, there is a good deal of judgment involved for most maintenance tasks, there is still a good deal of art involved in the application of crafts rather than science alone, and—last but not least—most maintenance workers consider themselves a cut above most plant workers and resent the intrusion of management control systems in their work similar to control systems the ordinary plant operator is exposed to.

For all of these reasons alone, control is important. In fact, a maintenance organization exposed to the discipline of effective control techniques costs significantly less to operate when compared to an uncontrolled department. That is a matter of record.

Figure 16-1 is an example of a weekly report Houston uses to control labor performance in its maintenance department.

The first two columns indicate the type of craft and the number of people in each craft while the third column lists the hours each craft and the entire department worked during the week.

The next two columns show just how many of these hours worked were spent on planned activities for both routine and preventive maintenance (P.M.). Planned activities, in hours, are those activities planned ahead of time by maintenance supervisors to which work standards have been applied.*

The next column, "Unscheduled" reflects those hours spent on emergency and unplanned maintenance work. Adding this column to the two previous columns under "Planned Hours" results in the hours listed in the "Total Hours Worked" column.

"Earned Hours," the next column, shows hours earned on work standards. The next column, "% Labor Performance" is derived by dividing earned hours by planned hours, as seen here:

$$\% \text{ Labor Performance} = \frac{\text{Earned Hours}}{\text{Routine} + \text{P.M. Hours}} \times 100$$

The final column shows how much time was actually spent on hours being measured by work standards. Since hours on work standards is equivalent to planned hours, time on standards is derived like this:

$$\% \text{ of Time on Standards} = \frac{\text{Routine} + \text{P.M. Hours}}{\text{Total Hours Worked.}} \times 100$$

Notice that only 57.3% of all maintenance time was spent on planned work with work standards. This is not unusual. The object, of course, is

*See Chapters 4 and 5 for an explanation of work standards applications.

INTERNATIONAL MACHINERY, INC.
PARTS MANUFACTURING DIVISION
MAINTENANCE LABOR REPORT

Plant: Houston

Week Ending: 3/24/81

CRAFT	NUMBER OF MEN	TOTAL HOURS WORKED	PLANNED HOURS ROUTINE	PLANNED HOURS P.M.	UNSCHEDULED HOURS	EARNED HOURS	% LABOR PERFORMANCE	% OF TIME ON STDS.
Machinists	10	430	205	40	185	220	89.8	60.0
General maintenance	6	210	180		30	190	105.6	85.7
Electricians	6	240	100	40	100	130	92.9	58.3
Pipefitters	4	130	60		70	50	83.3	46.2
Truck mechanics	2	80			80			
Total department	28	1090	545	80	465	580	92.8	57.3

Figure 16-1. Parts Manufacturing Division: Maintenance labor report.

to approach 100%—but it will never quite be reached because the nature of maintenance work is that emergencies will always occur, and that emergency work is unplanned and essentially hard to measure for work standards.

Returning to labor performance, it can be stated that 92.8% for the entire department is a respectable performance, and that an examination of labor performance for individual crafts does not reveal any exceptionally poor performances, although the 83.3% performance of the pipefitters, and 89.8% performance for machinists can certainly be improved.

SCHEDULES MISSED

Analysis of the maintenance labor report is likely to indicate areas of performance which management will want to examine closely. An ancillary report to aid them in this task is called the "Schedules Missed" report as illustrated by a cutaway in Figure 16-2.

This report automatically prints out those work orders whose earned labor performance falls below a stated percentage. Houston management selected 90% as the lowest percentage it considers acceptable performance. Any work order performance level slipping below that point is programmed to be displayed on a computer report automatically.

The Schedules Missed report describes work order performance as contrasted to the maintenance labor report which describes labor per-

INTERNATIONAL MACHINERY, INC.
PARTS MANUFACTURING DIVISION
SCHEDULES MISSED REPORT
FOR
MAINTENANCE WORK ORDERS

Plant: Houston   Week Ending: 3/24/81

WORK ORDER NUMBER	WORK DESCRIPTION	PLANNED HOURS	EARNED HOURS	% LABOR PERFORMANCE
80-12	Repair 6″ drill press	50	40	80.0
80-28	Install monorail system	121	86	71.1
80-34	Rebush boring mill	168	122	72.6

Figure 16-2. Parts Manufacturing Division: Schedule missed report.

INTERNATIONAL MACHINERY, INC.
PARTS MANUFACTURING DIVISION
CRAFTSMAN PERFORMANCE REPORT

Plant: Houston   Week Ending: 3/24/81

| | CURRENT WEEK PERFORMANCE | | | | YTD PERFORMANCE | |
CRAFTSMAN NAME	PLANNED HOURS	EARNED HOURS	% LABOR PERFORMANCE	% OF TIME ON STDS.	% LABOR PERFORMANCE	% OF TIME ON STDS.
Jones	32	30	93.8	80.0	91.7	51.5
Rawlins	18	16	88.9	45.0	90.5	46.7
Fanton	22	17	77.3	55.0	86.9	48.3

Figure 16-3. Parts Manufacturing Division: Craftsman performance report.

formance by craft. Between the two, maintenance management is given sufficient information to detect weak spots, make corrections, and control overall performance. Both reports, then, attack collective labor performance from different angles.

The schedules missed report starts with a listing of the delinquent work order numbers and a description of the tasks contained in the work orders. It then goes on to list planned hours, earned hours, and percent labor performance as shown in the maintenance labor report.

CRAFTSMAN PERFORMANCE

While the maintenance labor performance report and the schedules missed report focus on overall work order and departmental labor performance, the craftsman performance report details individual craftsman performance. Figure 16-3 is an example of such a report used by Houston.

The left-hand column lists each craftsman's name, and the following columns calculate his labor performance and percent of time on standards for both the current week and year-to-date (YTD). This report shows maintenance supervisors which craftsmen need additional training and direction. The YTD columns allow supervisors to track individual performance over the course of the year. Craftsman Ferguson, for example, had a labor performance of 77.3% for the current week and is only at 86.9% for the current year—a poor performance. Obviously, Ferguson is in need of some supervisory attention.

INTERNATIONAL MACHINERY, INC.
PARTS MANUFACTURING DIVISION
YTD MACHINE MAINTENANCE COSTS

Plant: Houston   Week Ending: 3/24/81

MACHINE	MAINTENANCE LABOR COSTS	MATERIAL COSTS	TOTAL COSTS	REPLACEMENT COSTS
Grinder # 2R	$280.50	$ 6.75	$287.25	$12500.00
Miller # 3F	660.35	225.30	885.65	16750.00
Tapper # 4G	106.50	85.90	192.40	17200.00
Reamer # 7T	675.90	910.32	1586.22	10900.00

Figure 16-4. Parts Manufacturing Division: Machine maintenance costs.

MACHINE MAINTENANCE COSTS

Houston's machine maintenance costs report is shown in Figure 16-4. This report shows how much it costs to maintain individual pieces of production (or support) machinery. The columns of the report show, from left to right, machine, labor costs, materials costs, total costs, and replacement costs. By comparing total costs with replacement costs, manufacturing and maintenance managers can determine when the purchase of new machinery is more economical than repairing existing machinery.

This report also helps managers spot developing problems in machinery. It helps managers recognize the principle that when maintenance costs increase so does machine downtime and that maintenance costs can be reduced significantly when machinery failures are minimized. Smart maintenance managers recognize that a thorough preventive maintenance operation on production machinery coupled with the replacement of parts which exhibit high failure rates are the prime ingredients in the reduction of machinery maintenance costs.

17
Establishing and Controlling a Cost Reduction Program

"Creative thinking may mean simply the realization that there's no particular virture in doing things the way they always have been done."

Rudolf Flesch

Every manufacturing manager is aware of the fact that, where costs are concerned, to stand still is to die! Labor costs increase with the signing of every labor contract, purchased parts are priced higher every year, and other related manufacturing costs continue to climb. Yet the company's profit plan aims at higher margins annually.

To counter the cost spiral it is essential that manufacturing organizations pursue cost reduction aggresively. It is imperative that an organized cost reduction program be in place, that it be ongoing, and that it be productive. The cost reduction effort should report organizationally to the manufacturing manager to impress employees with its importance and to ensure that the program is reducing significant costs. A good approach is to appoint a cost reduction coordinator who would work at the cost reduction program full time. His job would be to review cost reduction proposals, calculate cost savings impact, and provide management with written reports concerning progress of the program.

To get the program moving, every section of manufacturing—production, materials, quality control, and manufacturing engineering—would establish cost reduction goals thay can achieve and have those goals approved by the manufacturing manager. A total goal for manufacturing would then be established and incorporated within the company's annual profit plan. Progress to the goal would be followed monthly for individual departments.

PMD's Los Angeles plant has such a cost reduction program with a goal of $1 million annual cost savings and an effective cost savings rate of $500,000. An effective cost savings is that portion of an annual cost savings that is actually achieved for the calendar year. If, for example, a proposal to rework obsolete parts so they can be used in current production is estimated to save $10,000 annually, and the proposal is actually implemented half-way through the year, then the effective cost savings would be $5000.

One device that has been found to be particularly effective in encouraging active participation in the cost reduction program is a conspicuously posted board showing the results to-date of the program. Los Angeles' board is shown in Figure 17-1.

The value of posting results for everybody to see is that most employees are sensitive to the approval of their peers as well as their bosses. When everybody knows what everybody else is doing—or not doing—there is a subtle impetus to make the best showing possible.

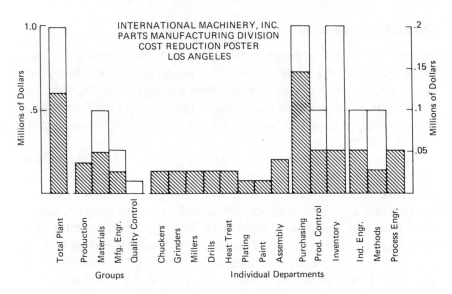

Figure 17-1. Parts Manufacturing Division: cost reduction poster.

The cost reduction board illustrated in Figure 17-1 is divided into three sections: "Groups," "Individual Departments," and "Total Plant."

The length of each bar on the chart signifies the goal in dollars for each individual department, as well as group and plant totals. The shaded area within each bar is an indication of annual cost savings achieved year-to-date. (Annual savings are posted, not effective savings). Since half the year has gone by, roughly half of each bar should be shaded. Those that aren't show that cost savings goals are not being achieved in concert with the plan.

There are two scales for the chart. The dollar scale at the left pertains to "Total Plant" and "Groups." This scale goes to $1 million. The scale on the right is for individual departments and goes to $200,000. The right-hand scale was added so bars for individual departments were large enough to observe on the graph.

Los Angeles has their cost reduction board posted at the entrance to the employees' cafeteria where it is visible to all eyes. The board is ten feet wide and four feet high and enclosed in a glass case. Its conspicuous location has generated a great deal of interest in the program.

EVALUATION OF COST SAVINGS PROPOSALS

In any cost reduction program there will be a multitude of proposals made. Some of these will be workable, and some will not. Many proposals will deal with cost control as opposed to cost reduction. Cost control proposals are not true cost savings. They suggest the limitation of costs to budgetary dollars; as such they do not propose to reduce costs, only to hold them in line.

Workable cost reduction ideas generally deal in true elimination: elimination of a part, a material, an operation, an employee. Other productive cost savings can be achieved in part substitution (using a cheaper part or substituting obsolete inventory), combining operations, or use of new machinery capable of higher production rates than machinery now being used. The better cost reduction proposals focus on areas where costs are high. It takes as much effort, for example, to cut 10% off a $100,000 part as it does to cut 10% off a $10,000 part.

Cost savings proposals must be thoroughly investigated to assure their ability to do the job. Los Angeles organizes this effort through a cost reduction proposal seen in Figure 17-2. An example of a proposal is illustrated using their cost reduction proposal form. Sections "A," "B," "C," and "D" are self explanatory.

Section "E" describes the dollars to be saved if the proposal is accepted, and it also shows the costs of implementation. "Payback" refers to the length of time capital costs and expenses needed to imple-

---

PARTS MANUFACTURING DIVISION
COST REDUCTION PROPOSAL

A | Plant: *LOS ANGELES* | Originator: *J. MURPHY*
Part Number: *PMD-163* | Part Name: *2 ¼" BRACKET*

B | Proposal: *REMILL SLOT ON BRACKET SO IT CAN BE USED FOR 2 ¼" BRACKET, THEREBY USING 2 ¼" BRACKETS WHICH HAVE BEEN SITTING IN INVENTORY FOR THREE YEARS.*

C | Current Method: *2 ½" BRACKETS ARE CURRENTLY BEING USED.*

D | Cost Savings: *THERE ARE 20,000 OF THE 2 ¼" BRACKETS NOW IN INVENTORY. CONVERTING THESE TO 2 ½" BRACKETS—A FULL YEARS SUPPLY—WOULD RESULT IN A COST SAVINGS OF $10,000 (THE 2 ½" BRACKETS COST $0.50 EACH).*

E | Payback: *ABOUT THREE WEEKS* Annual Cost Savings: *$10,000*
Capital Costs: *NONE* Effective Cost Savings: *$5,000 -SIX MONTHS*
Expense: *REWORK COSTS OF $540* Project Completion Date: *2 WEEKS -6/30/81*

F | Approvals: Manufacturing Manager *M. Johnson* Date: *6/12/81*
Quality Manager _____ Date: *6/13/81*
Accountant _____ Date: *6/13/81*
Cost Reduction Coordinator _____ Date: *6/10/81*
Plant Manager *R. Brown* Date: *6/12/81*

Figure 17-2. Parts Manufacturing Division: cost reduction proposal.

ment the proposal will be balanced by the cost savings achieved. In the example shown the payback is about three weeks:

$$\text{Weekly Cost Savings} = \frac{\text{Annual Savings}}{52 \text{ Weeks}} = \frac{\$10,000}{52 \text{ Weeks}} = \$192$$

$$\text{Payback} = \frac{\text{Implementation Costs}}{\text{Weekly Savings}} = \frac{\$540}{\$192} = 2.8 \text{ Weeks}$$

Implementation costs in the example refer to the combination of both capital costs and expenses.

Section "F" is reserved for approval sign-offs of the proposal. It is always a good idea to include the quality control manager in the sign-off process. Many times proposals are made to reduce costs which totally ignore the impact of poor quality. A material substitution, for example, may save thousands of dollars initially but may cause failures of the product in use, and the savings will be wiped out through high warranty costs.

18
Safety Control

"No one is useless in this world who lightens the burdens of another."
Charles Dickens

There is no need to argue the case for safety; it's hard to conceive of a manufacturing manager who isn't convinced. Yet the manufacturing manager many times has a slippery hold on the safety reins. Too often he does not know how to control safety, and he then drops the reins in the safety professional's hands.

Unfortunately, that is tantamount to losing control. While the safety man will do his best and exercise his considerable safety expertise, it will not be enough. The manufacturing manager needs to get involved. It is his interest in the safety program and his direction of safety efforts that will produce a safety-conscious environment.

There are three basic reports which place control of safety securely in the manufacturing managers hands, all of which are easily handled by a computer. These are:

1. The lost time and accident report.
2. The accident type report
3. The operator frequency report

THE LOST TIME AND ACCIDENT REPORT

This report summarizes both accident and lost time statistics for manufacturing. Figure 18-1 is a reproduction of PMD Houston's lost time and accident report.

The left-hand column lists all of Houston's departments where hourly employees work. (The report does not include salaried people; it purports to control hourly employee safety performance alone. A separate report is issued for salaried employee safety).

The next two columns list the number of accidents experienced by each department for both the current year and past year YTD. This comparison gives management the opportunity to detect unwholesome safety trends.

The following two columns contrast the number of man-hours lost due to work-related injuries by department for both the current year and past year YTD. In some respects lost time is more meaningful than accidents alone. Lost time attests to the relative seriousness of injuries and, as such, it is a qualitative factor. One department may exhibit, for example, several minor accidents for the quarter while another department may have experienced but one injury for the same period. If that single injury, however, resulted in a lost limb it would most obviously rate more corrective action attention than the department which had the minor accidents.

INTERNATIONAL MACHINERY, INC.
PARTS MANUFACTURING DIVISION
LOST TIME AND ACCIDENT REPORT[1]
3/81 YTD

DEPARTMENT	NUMBER OF ACCIDENTS		MAN-HOURS LOST TIME		LOST TIME RATE[2]	
	3/81 YTD	3/80 YTD	3/81 YTD	3/80 YTD	3/81 YTD	3/80 YTD
Grinders	3	2	168	0		
Drill presses	0	1	0	40		
Millers	2	3	0	32		
Chuckers	1	0	16	0		
Screw machines	4	2	480	0		
Heat treat	2	0	8	0		
Production control	3	4	0	176		
Quality control	0	3	0	240		
Mfg. engineering	6	7	132	216		
Total Plant	21	23	804	704	.005	.007

1. Hourly employees only

2. Lost Time Rate $= \dfrac{\text{Number of Man-Hours Lost Time}}{\text{Number of Man-Hours Worked}}$

Figure 18-1. Parts Manufacturing Division: Lost time and accident report.

The accident rate, moreover, is sometimes a harbinger of things to come. Lost time injuries are many times heralded by a series of minor accidents. When many small accidents occur it is many times an indication of insufficient attention to safety by both hourly and salaried employees.

The final two columns list the lost time rate for equal periods, this year and last year. The lost time rate is found by dividing the number of man-hours of lost time by the number of man-hours worked during the period. In this case, Houston has elected to define the lost time rate for the total plant only, but it could have been easily determined on a department-by-department basis.

Notice that while lost time man-hours were greater for the current period (804 man-hours) than for the preceding year (704 man-hours), the lost time rate was lower for the current year (.005 vs. .007). This is because more man-hours have been worked during the first quarter of 1981 as compared with the first quarter of 1980.

THE ACCIDENT TYPE REPORT

It is always helpful to know those kind of accidents most prevalent in the plant. An analysis of Figure 18-2 reveals a pattern of injuries for PMD Houston. Strains, constitute by far, the most frequent category of

INTERNATIONAL MACHINERY, INC.
PARTS MANUFACTURING DIVISION
ACCIDENT TYPES
3/81 YTD

CATEGORY OF INJURIES	YEAR-TO-DATE 1981	1980
Fall or slip	5	2
Strain	11	10
Skin rashes	3	1
Moving vehicle accident	1	3
Struck by or struck against	1	4
Caught in or between	0	3
Total	21	23

Figure 18-2. Parts Manufacturing Division: Accident types.

injuries. Falls or slips (a related type of injury to strains) is the second largest category. From this information Houston management is now in a position to take effective corrective action. Their next step would be to examine the history of each type of injury to determine if any additional pattern exists. Some departments, for instance, may be more susceptible to strain and fall or slip injuries than others. Effective corrective action can then focus on specific areas for improvement.

THE OPERATOR FREQUENCY REPORT

A final but important report issued by safety functions is the operator frequency report. This type of report pinpoints so-called "accident prone" employees. In most manufacturing environments, certain individuals will suffer more accidents than others. Those employees, in almost all cases, are people who are careless and who haven't had the benefit of safety training. A discovery of who those employees are allows management the opportunity to work with affected employees, teaching

INTERNATIONAL MACHINERY, INC.
PARTS MANUFACTURING DIVISION
OPERATOR FREQUENCY REPORT

NAME	TYPE OF ACCIDENT	DATE OF ACCIDENT	LOST TIME
Johnson, Mark	Strain	2/15/81	8 Hours
	Strain	6/12/80	40 Hours
	Cut hand	2/25/79	None
	Slipped on oil	7/3/77	80 Hours
	Strain	9/18/75	120 Hours
	Bruised hand	3/16/72	None
	Slipped on oil	10/2/71	32 Hours

Employee Number:	1055	
Seniority Date:	12/5/70	
History:	Material Handler, Machine Shop	12/5/70—4/10/72
	Grinder Operator	4/11/72—7/20/80
	Drill Press Operator	7/20/80—Current

Figure 18-3. Parts Manufacturing Division: Operator frequency report.

them positive safety practices. Figure 18-3 is such a report used by Houston to spot the problem employees.

This report, like the other safety reports before it, is suited perfectly for the computer. Programmed properly, the employee's name or number can be punched into a terminal and the type of information shown in Figure 18-3 is then readily available. Notice that *all* accidents during the employee's entire time with the company are listed.

19
Labor Relations

"The aim is not more goods for people to buy, but more opportunities for them to live."

Lewis Mumford

Good labor relations is not entirely the province of industrial relations experts; the manufacturing manager's job is greatly affected by the morale of people in the plants. If employees are generally content, production remains high and costs low. If employees are basically dissatisfied then production problems are bound to erupt. The life of a manufacturing manager is difficult enough without the creation of severe morale problems on the factory floor. He has to contend with production schedules, costs, quality, safety, and an entire host of related factors which could bring most men to their knees. If, on top of all these problems, the results of poor morale are superimposed, his job becomes practically untenable.

Labor relations can be controlled. But first the manufacturing manager needs to be aware of certain trends in the plants; these trends are:

1. Absenteeism and Tardiness
2. Grievances
3. Discipline

ABSENTEEISM AND TARDINESS

This is one of the most imposing problems facing almost all manufacturing operations today. For different reasons, employees miss a lot of

164

PARTS MANUFACTURING DIVISION WEEKLY ABSENTEE REPORT				PLANT: HOUSTON	WEEK ENDING:4/15	
ABSENTEE/TARDY CATEGORY	GRINDING	DRILL PRESSES	MILLERS	CHUCKERS	SCREW MACHINES	HEAT TREAT	TOTAL PLANT
Late punch-in	2			1	3		6
Early punch-out		4		3	2	1	10
No call in	1	1				2	4
Union Business			1				1
Death in family							0
Personal excuse	2	1		1	2	1	7
Disciplinary action				5			5
Jury duty							0
Totals	5	6	1	10	7	4	33

Figure 19-1. Parts Manufacturing Division: Weekly absentee report.

time from work. The job of the manufacturing manager here is not to solve the absentee problem itself (that enormous undertaking is under study by a myriad group of behavioral psychologists) but to keep track of the absentee rate and begin investigating significant deviations from the norm. If, for example, the absentee rate at a plant is averaging 5%, and suddenly it jumps to 10%, that would be an indication that something radical has occurred to change conditions. A thorough analysis of the problem at that stage may prevent a catastrophic increase in the absentee rate.

Figure 19-1 shows Houston's weekly absentee report for the factory's production workers (separate reports are made for both salaried people and indirect labor). The left side of the report lists categories of absenteeism and tardiness and the other columns show actual numbers of absent or tardy employees by department for the week. Houston summarizes all of its absenteeism and tardiness for all people in a report similar to the one shown in Figure 19-1. The essential statistics are shown here:

WEEK ENDING: 4/15

	4/15	YTD	LAST YEAR
Salaried	4.3%	3.5%	3.8%
Hourly direct	17.4%	8.7%	8.9%
Hourly indirect	6.6%	6.0%	6.4%
Total Plant	11.6%	7.6%	7.9%

Quite obviously something went haywire in the absenteeism rate for hourly direct employees, during the current week. These kind of data allow manufacturing managers to be alert to trends and places them in favorable positions for taking effective corrective action before the problems become inordinately serious.

GRIEVANCES AND DISCIPLINE

These subjects are related. The issuance of discipline in the plants will generally, although not always, generate grievances.

The number of grievances submitted is usually a fairly reliable indicator of the morale of people in the factory. Generally, the more the number of grievances issued the more prevalent the unresolved issues affecting the morale of employees.

A workforce exhibiting high morale usually submits a low number of grievances (except around contract negotiation time when the union deliberately sponsors all the grievances it can get to use as wedges during contract negotiations).

When the number of grievances submitted is high, *and when many of them focus on similar complaints,* you can bet there are serious,

INTERNATIONAL MACHINERY, INC.
PARTS MANUFACTURING DIVISION
GRIEVANCES AND DISCIPLINE

Plant: Houston   Week Ending: 6/26/80

GRIEVANCES			DISCIPLINE	
THIS WEEK	YTD		THIS WEEK	YTD
0	2	Grinders	0̶0̶	0̶0̶
2	3	Drill presses	1̶3̶	1̶3̶
0	0	Millers	0̶0̶	0̶0̶
0	0	Chuckers	1̶0̶	2̶1̶
1	4	Screw machines	0̶0̶	1̶F̶
0	1	Heat treat	0̶0̶	1̶0̶
2	6	Support depts.	2̶4̶	3̶5̶
5	16	TOTAL PLANT	4 7	8 9 plus one F[1]

[1]Employee terminated for stealing company property.

Figure 19-2. Parts Manufacturing Division: Grievances and discipline.

unresolved problems with the workforce. The longer these fester the more liable they are to ultimately result in poor quality, poor production, and higher accident rates. When people face problems to which there are no apparent solutions, their minds seldom stay long on the jobs at hand.

Figure 19-2 is divided into two sections. The left-hand section describes grievances for PMD's Houston plant. For the first six months of the year sixteen grievances have been submitted. This is not a large number of grievances when you consider that Houston has about 340 hourly people.

The right-hand side of Figure 19-2 displays the number of times disciplinary action was taken and days-off issued during the first half of 1980. The numbers on top of the diagonal lines show the actual number of disciplinary actions taken. The numbers below the diagonal lines show days-off without pay for employees receiving disciplinary action. In regard to Houston's workforce, the amount and severity of disciplinary actions do not appear to be excessive.

Index

Index

Index